Desert Roots
Journey of an Iranian Immigrant Family

Desert Roots
Journey of an Iranian Immigrant Family

Mitra Karbassi Shavarini

LFB Scholarly Publishing LLC
El Paso 2012

Library of Congress Cataloging-in-Publication Data

Shavarini, Mitra K., 1962-
  Desert roots : journey of an Iranian immigrant family / Mitra Karbassi
Shavarini.
    p. cm.
  Includes bibliographical references and index.
  ISBN 978-1-59332-499-5 (pbk. : alk. paper)
  1. Iranian Americans--Biography. 2. Iranian Americans--Cultural
assimilation. 3. Karbassi family. 4. Shavarini, Mitra K., 1962---
Family. 5. Immigrants--Family relationships--United States. 6. Return
migration--Iran. 7. Place attachment. 8. Iran--Biography. I. Title.
  E184.I5S428 2012
  305.89155'073--dc23
                                    2012014673

ISBN 978-1-59332-499-5

Printed on acid-free 250-year-life paper.

Manufactured in the United States of America.

To Neemah & Donya

Sabine & Niku

Kiana & Shayan

Contents

Acknowledgements

I am deeply grateful to friends who have proffered support, enthusiasm and advice throughout the writing of this book: Merce Crosas, Marie-Aude Hewes, Francis Hurley, Farnaz Shemirani, Helen Snively, Karen Virk, and Juliette Zenner. For their thought-provoking feedback, I am thankful to John Adams, Elizabeth Harvey and Margaret Moody. For the editing know-how that shaped this story into a book, I thank Dan Hunter, Dody Riggs, Heather Mitchell, and Veronica Golos. Of course, none of this effort would have been possible without Hadi. His ever-constant reminder that I am writing this for our children kept me going when the past was too difficult to re-visit. And finally my parents, Akhtar and Reza Karbassi, whose decision to return home opened an illuminating door to our family's past. Baba, I wish you had a chance to read "your" last chapter.

Desert Roots

With the clear and disciplined eyes of an ethnographer, the storytelling and perspective-taking of a historian, the art and economy of a poet, and the deep devotion of a daughter, Mitra Shavarini traces four generations of an Iranian family transplanted, but never at home, in America. Capturing the treacherous journeys across time and place, the stubborn resistance to assimilation, and the complex identities defined by gender and generation, *Desert Roots* is ultimately a beautiful story about the resilience and endurance of the human spirit.

> Sara Lawrence-Lightfoot
> Professor, Harvard University
> Author of *Balm in Gilead*,
> *Respect*, and *The Third Chapter*

Reminiscent of the immortal 13th century Persian mystical poet, Rumi and his story of the reed, Mitra Shavarini's *Desert Roots* tells of the anguish of separation and the ever-intensifying desire for return – return to one's "origin." Whether it is her parents' desire to return to Iran in their old age, her mother's marriage at a young age against her desire to continue with her education, or her father's loss of parents and a younger brother, Shavarini's poignant stories of family separation from their roots, or estrangement from each other, struck a very familiar cord. Over and over again, in these poignant stories, the reader identifies with different existential dilemmas as Shavarini's life history unfolds. Written with honesty and elegance, Shavarini has woven an attractive tapestry of the lives of her family within the context of Iranian history and culture, itself having gone through its story of upheavals and separation. I could not put this book down.

Shahla Haeri
Associate Professor of Anthropology
Boston University
Author of *No Shame for the Sun: Lives of Professional Pakistani Women*, and *Law of Desire: Temporary Marriage, Mut'a, in Iran*

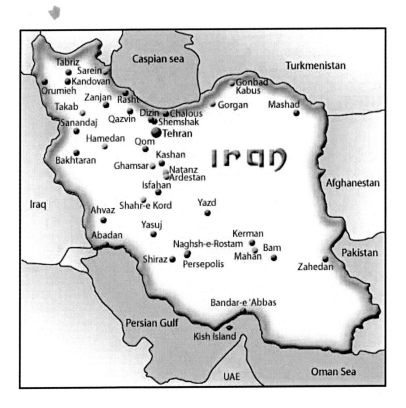

Perhaps deep in her—perhaps deep in every being—there lingers a desire to bring the circle of life back to its starting point . . .

—Abraham Verghese, *Cutting for Stone*

Introduction

It was my mother who gave me the news: after thirty-three years, they were going back home to Iran. She told me my father had made his decision.

I had always sensed my parents' connection to Iran, but it never occurred to me that they would yield to the calling of their birthplace. The Iran they had left three decades earlier wasn't the same Iran that exists today. I asked myself why my father would decide it was time to go back, especially considering the fact that his damnation of the Islamic government that had replaced the Persian monarchy, and of the clerics who forced him into self-exile, was a daily occurrence in our household.

Immigrants like my parents, who long to one day return to their homeland, more often than not pine for a country that no longer exists. They become exiles not of one land but of two countries.

Why does an immigrant, even one who, like my father, a proud naturalized U.S. citizen, decide it's time to go back home? What propels them back to their country of origin? When does the feeling of homeland become all consuming, its call too difficult to ignore?

Within these pages lies my quest to understand my father's decision to return to Iran—the whys, the hows—which ultimately led me to trace our family history. The story is of a uniquely Iranian experience—of the home culture, of rootedness, and of exile. It is a story of Iran beyond the Revolution, beyond politics—the story of an Iranian family whose tradition of endurance reaches back centuries. It is a story I hope my children will pass on to theirs.

I hold my hand out and invite you to join me in my parents' journey to—and eventually from—America.

Mitra K. Shavarini

Chapter 1
Ghorbat

Neither am I happy in Ghorbat, nor in my homeland
O'God. I hope fate turns this dark destiny of mine.

—Persian proverb

Farsi is a language of subtleties, thus there is no exact English translation for the Persian word *ghorbat:* nostalgia, exile, longing for homeland, feeling yourself a stranger is close to the idea. To truly understand ghorbat, one must live the word, feel its burden. It is one of those intangibles, like heartache, or when you realize you are lost. Yearning

I'm nine years old. I am wearing a neatly ironed private school uniform, white ankle socks, and shiny patent leather shoes my mother bought me in one of those fancy stores in downtown Tehran. A circle of twenty girls surrounds me, all shrieking with delight. It's my last day at Ravesh Noa, a private girls' school. Started by Anoshirvan Rohani, a modern musician and songwriter, and modeled after Western schools, Ravesh Noa is the rage among the sliver of society that now constitutes Iran's middle class. Since my father has already left the country, a driver from his company has come to pick me up. I have a hard time making my way through the little bodies who all want to touch "the girl who is lucky enough to go to America."

Twenty years later, I dream of my maternal grandmother. She waits behind a glass door. Her hair is pulled back, tight at the part. She wears a weathered sweater that reminds me of mothballs. It's the color of embers, that particular glow right before they turn to ash. Before it fades, like memory, my grandmother says, "I see you." From the other side of the glass I stare at the lines on her face, shaped and grooved like destiny. I cannot open the glass door between us. I wake up in tears. Furious.

Ghorbat.

Narragansett
2005

She stands in the cluttered garage surrounded by boxes, holding a dusty and long untouched ceramic bowl, a school project her daughter made in the fourth grade. She has kept this clay piece, roughly shaped by little fingers, for many years. Year after year she has put the stuff of her life into boxes, thinking one day she may want them. That someday never came. Instead, she finds herself picking through boxes, meeting strange memories. She is convinced that, at seventy-four years of age, it is now time to put her boxes in order.

She traces where her daughter's fingers had been thirty-three years earlier. She feels again the simple joy she felt the day her daughter brought home this shiny, glazed-hardened earth from school, proud to show off her handicraft. She had a dishtowel in her hands when her daughter danced into the kitchen. She remembers thinking, *How lucky my girl is to go to school while we're in America.* On that day she told her daughter, "Your path in life will be different from mine."

Now, standing in her garage, she feels that she can taste the memory. She almost feels she can taste the little clay bowl—a tormenting mixture of fondness and sadness. She wants to spit it out . . . or hold it in. She doesn't know. So many things stir in her heart.

Yes, her daughter's path has been different, different from her own mother's, too. And her path has been different from what she had dreamed. Standing in an American garage in suburban Rhode Island, she feels that she is at the end of two paths, two sets of memories: one in America and one in Iran. Some of these boxes hold memories of Iran, and some of her life in America.

Her little girl's bowl is America

Thirty-three years ago they came to America. The move was meant to be temporary . . . at least that's what they assumed. She never imagined that they would become exiles from Iran. Isolated and alone—exiles from America itself. Their days turned into years, and years into old age. She lets out a loud sigh, so loud that it screams with pain.

"Is it really time to go back?" she asks herself. Then, pausing a moment, she adds, "home." She feels glad but uncertain. Even her husband grudgingly agrees that their exile from Iran has come to an end. In these final years of life, the call of Iran—their land—has become too strong to ignore. She feels that the very earth of their homeland is pulling them back, drawing her and her husband back to join their ancestors. Just as her daughter dug her small hands into the wet American clay that would shape her life in this country, she longs to be back on the ground worked by her people, by her ancestors. She thinks of her father learning the Tayamom from the Koran: in the absence of water we are cleansed by God's earth, and the rock along the road becomes the prayer stone. Perhaps it is the duty of Persians to return home. Perhaps we will be washed clean by the soil of Iran.

In the few months since their decision to return home became final, she has been bringing items from the upstairs rooms into the garage and going through them one by one. Piled in boxes are photographs, letters, awards, souvenirs, gifts, and art projects. She feels nothing has been worth keeping, but nothing can easily be thrown away either. As she inspects each item, memories wash over her. She feels a need to forget, to let go. But she is afraid to obliterate her family's history. *Their* personal journey, painstakingly etched. What will her six grandchildren, who barely speak Farsi, understand of their origins? Of the lives and events that brought them here? How could she ever tell them, in her broken English, of their past? Won't they need strong roots to feel secure and certain about who they are? She hesitates to throw anything in the waste bin. Is she wiping away *their* past along with her own?

On this early July morning, she has pulled up the garage door to let in some fresh air. The sun has begun rising over the small coastal town of Narragansett, in Rhode Island. Two neighbors dressed in colorful warm-up outfits and bright white sneakers pass her driveway with exaggerated strides. She often sees these two women. They don't say hello. They don't even see her. In Iran, you would not just walk by a neighbor. She thinks how different they are from one another, she and they, how in all her years in Narragansett she has lived in a world apart from theirs. She observes the two women's rapid gaits; engaged in conversation, they seem confident. Relaxed. She wonders whether they are gossiping, whether they have a friendship in which they commiserate, laugh, and share thoughts and dreams. She watches them until they are distant dots, feeling a wave of emptiness wash over her. Two strangers remind her of her strangeness in this land—even after thirty-three years. She sighs deeply, then turns over the ceramic bowl she is still holding in her hand. Inscribed underneath in the unglazed clay is "MK 72." She stares at her daughter's initials, at the year that held so much promise. Cupped in her hand, the ceramic bowl waits to be bidden farewell, to be set free from the chambers of her heart. For a woman who defines herself by her devotion to motherhood, throwing away the clay bowl is a dilemma riddled with anguish. She murmurs to herself, "You did your duty as a mother, *vel kon,* let go," then brushes her hand—over and over—across the ceramic's rough edges before gently placing it in the garbage bin. A proper farewell before letting it go.

She wonders if coming to the United States has been worth all that they've been through: all the years of uncertainty, humiliation, struggling, toil. She has sown seed on a foreign land. Will she be here for the harvest? Can she leave just when her sacrifices are beginning to bear fruit? It's not easy to go, she admits to herself, but how can she stay? The question nags at her, she fights to keep her emotions together. To sedate the dull ache crushing her heart, she reminds herself of her children's successes. Each has a life here they can be proud of: homes, families, friends, and jobs. They have lives that make them belong. She does not . . . she never did.

She pulls out a photograph that until recently graced the front entrance hallway of their home. Large and conspicuous, it pointed proudly to a grand moment in the family's life. It was the first thing one would see upon entering the house and was difficult to ignore—unless you had walked by it every day for thirty-three years. To her it had become invisible: a familiar sight that faded into its white background. But now, in the garage, she sees it as if for the first time—maybe due to the clarity of the morning light. The black and white photograph was taken some fifty years earlier at what was a great event for Iran—the opening of a new oil refinery. She sees a line of five men in dark suits, white shirts, and thin, tightly knotted ties. The man at the head of the line is bending forward with his eyes closed to reverently kiss the outstretched hand of a square-shouldered man, the Shah. This is an image of the monarch and his obedient subjects. The one bending is her husband. The Shah's gaze is empty. The four other men, like her husband, are young managers for the National Iranian Oil Company, who wait their turn behind her husband's bent back.

The men standing behind the Shah all wear the same dark suits, white shirts, and skinny dark ties, but their eyes are hidden behind dark sunglasses. Bodyguards.

She looks closely at the eyes of each of the men standing at attention and sees respect. Obedience. Trepidation. All emotions born of fear. She remembers how everyone feared the Shah—his secret police, the torture, his anger at dissent, men disappearing in the night, freak accidents. Then she studies the face of the man bending forward with eyes closed to kiss the hand of the Shah, and she wonders if she knows this man. Has she *ever* known him, Reza Karbassi, her husband? She stares intently at her husband's face. A deep bow, eyes closed, his face so close to the Shah's right hand. Back then, she seems to remember, he was so proud, so full of hope.

She isn't sure what to do with the photograph. None of her children will want it. But it would be treasonous to take it back to Iran—the Revolutionary Guards will search for Western influences in every piece of luggage they bring into the country. She remembers the new government's blacklists at the dawn of the Revolution and the many friends they lost during the "cleansing" period. Even today, twenty-five years after the Revolution, any connection to the Shah could land you in jail. The photograph, she knows, just has no place in a country that has tried to wipe away its monarchy past, a country that now calls itself the "Islamic Republic."

She has no choice but to throw the photograph away. Yet, she hesitates to let go of this captured moment. She tries to convince herself that maybe, like anything captured, there comes a point at which it must be set free. Reluctantly, she reaches over to place the framed photograph next to the ceramic bowl in a half-filled rubbish bin, all the while gazing at her husband's reverent bow—a gesture of faith that the right kind of obedience will bring the right kind of life.

From inside the house she hears Reza calling: *"Khanom?"*

After fifty-five years of marriage he still calls her khanom, "lady" or "Mrs." in Farsi, and she calls him by his surname, Karbassi.

"In a minute," she responds. She retrieves the photograph from the bin and puts it back in a box. *For the time being,* she says to herself. Then she looks at the pile of stuff that still needs sifting through, things they won't be able to take back with them. Suddenly she feels overwhelmed.

"Khanom? Where is breakfast?" she hears Reza say again.

It is time to be obedient.

Slapping the dust off her blouse and skirt—to shed memories more than soil—she turns toward the door that leads inside the house. But thoughts of the photograph linger, shadowing her steps into the house like a ghost holding her hand, pulling her back in time.

As she walks down the dark hallway to her kitchen, her mind drifts back to when Reza was granted his four-year post with Sherkat Naft, the Iranian National Oil Company, or NIOC, as the Americans called it. To work at Sherkat Naft was a status symbol; it meant you were educated, modern, secular—a bureaucrat—and that life under the Shah served you well. That was Iran's new image: a burgeoning middle class that was being given access to upward social mobility. You could have a car and a TV to go with your white shirt and skinny tie.

Reza never fit that mold. He was far too honest and proud to steal and lie in order to get ahead, as did most of those around him. Yet Reza always wanted to claim the NIOC identity as his. Among his colleagues, she remembers, a four-year assignment to the U.S., typically awarded because of nepotism more than merit, was a bitterly sought-after position. In the new Iran, a foreign assignment was the golden egg. When her husband learned of his New York City post, he was certain of the bright future that this assignment—his second overseas—would create for his family. The day he received the official word, he came home with such a peppy stride that he was nearly skipping. She had never seen him filled with such childlike excitement.

"Our children will get the best education, an American education!" he beamed. "Oh, the lives they will have when they return to Iran."

The heavens had bestowed a gift. Nothing could be better than going to America; there was nothing to question, nothing to consider. Envied by friends and relatives, they were to pack up their lives in Tehran and go to live for four years in a land that enchanted her husband. It was more than the golden egg: Reza had found the goose that laid it.

"How many times do I have to call you?" Reza scolds from the stairwell, the master calling his servant. "What's taking you so long this morning?"

She knows better than to answer him. She continues toward the kitchen and thinks about when they first got to the States, to New York City. She and their three kids, aged nine to twenty, found their new lives difficult. Reza told them to put their focus on their schooling so they could return to Iran with as much education as their time here would afford them. Nothing, he drilled into them, was more important than their American education and the financial and social rewards it would bring them back in their country. He often said that the inconveniences they faced on foreign soil, away from family and friends, paled in the light of what they were gaining.

"Moman, they make fun of me all the time!" their thirteen-year-old son said to her one day. He had thought that Reza, watching the news in the adjoining room, wouldn't hear him complaining.

Before she could comfort her son, Reza blared from the other room, "*Chi gofti,* what did I hear you just say?"

Their quiet Forest Hills apartment shook. Her daughter ran out of the room. Her son trembled.

"Now you lose your tongue? *I* asked you a question. What is it that you are complaining about?" Reza said, hovering over their son's skinny teenage body.

Apprehensively, he replied, "Kids make fun of me. They mock me, like they say I am from 'I-ran' and then laugh."

Reza took out his belt and whipped it across his son's back in anger. "*Naw'shokr!* Ungrateful!"

None of them ever again spoke of the difficulties of their new lives in America.

"Breakfast will be ready in a minute, Karbassi," she says, swiftly walking through the hallway.

Inside her dark kitchen, she flips on the overhead lights. A pale glow fills the room. There is only one narrow window by the sink. It cranks open like an accordion fan. Even on the sunniest of days, this kitchen—with its walnut-colored cabinets and yellow Formica countertop—appears dark, like the cellar where her family kept chickens in her childhood. The 40-watt bulb barely sheds enough light to illuminate the entire space. She has never increased the wattage, fearing it would be wasteful and their electric bills would go up. Utilities are what she has been most careful of throughout their time in the States. When the government that overthrew the Shah froze their assets, she learned to watch every penny. She learned to sacrifice. And she, unlike Reza, learned not to look back and think about what they had lost. That is . . . until she started to bring their belongings into the garage and sort them in preparation for their trip back.

She arranges the table quickly and easily. Her husband's walk is slow and labored. The contrast between their movements brings into relief how out of sync they are with one another. She wonders if any couple exists with greater contrast. They are as different as fire from water; one is a burning flame, the other is a soothing flow. He shouts in anger while she remains silent. She sheds tears; he holds his back. He is as stubborn as she is acquiescent. As parents, he strikes with a hatchet of words that leaves lifetime wounds; she heals those blows with gently uttered proverbs. And around the house, she busies herself with one task after another, while he sits on his favorite yellow chair in the living room. She readily admits they have little in common, save their three children.

From the kitchen she can see Reza, struggling with his steps, slowly making his way down the hallway. He teeters down the dimly lit passage, mumbling *"chap, rast,* left, right . . ."
Watching him struggle, she wonders about this thing his doctor calls Parkinson's. Is it age? He's only five years older than she. His condition could be hereditary, but she knows better. Looking at his stooping, lumbering physique, she knows: it is the result of a lifetime of accumulated heartbreaks and disappointments.

"Right, left"—Reza makes his way toward the kitchen like a wound-up toy soldier.

She continues setting the breakfast table: his plate, followed by his medication bottles alongside a glass of water. She fills the tea kettle and slices her homemade bread. Reza stops and grabs the back of the chair as he tries to lower himself slowly and squarely in its middle.

Chapter 2
Eshgh

I never saw my parents hold hands, lock arms, or embrace one another. I never saw them kiss—save once. That was at Tehran's Mehrabad International Airport, the day Baba, my father, was leaving for the United States. He was going ahead to find us a place to live and get things ready for our arrival. I remember that Baba was so excited. Right before he went through the airline gate, he turned to my mother and put his lips to her cheek. A quick peck.

My parents never spoke in our presence about loving each other. Not that spoken Farsi allows for that. When you want to tell someone you love them, you don't use the word "love," *eshgh*. You say, *"Doost'et daram,"* "I like you." I've come to learn that the word "eshgh" is only used in our music, poetry, and literature. I read the works of our great poets—Rumi, Hafiz, Sa'adi, Khaayam—and notice that their writing is all about eshgh, romantic love. In Hafiz's poetry, wine is the metaphor for eshgh. His intoxication is not so much corporal but the divine: *Let thought become the beautiful woman . . . let prayer become your beautiful lover,* he writes. Page after page, song after song, verse after verse . . . I hear eshgh, I sense that my cultural background longs for eshgh . . . is infatuated with it. And yet, I never felt this eshgh between my parents.

13

In writing my parents' story, one of the questions I've asked myself is whether my parents ever loved one another. They must have. How could they have stayed together for so long—six decades—if they didn't? To find the answer, though, wasn't so easy. I had to explore the word "love," break it down to see what it meant . . . *to me*. I had to hold a mirror to myself and ask, Did *I* learn to love from my parents? How has their "eshgh-less" relationship shaped *my* understanding of love? To find the answer, I had to go back to my childhood . . . I had to go back to the beginning . . . to the desert.

What answers did I unearth?

Those, my reader, are hidden in these pages . . .

Kerman, Iran
1949

The Lut Desert is a 200-mile stretch of barren land, empty except for massive dunes, sand slopes and high ridges whipped into sword shapes by the fierce desert winds—forbidding terrain that has somehow harbored life for thousands of years. The fabled Silk Road crossed the Lut Desert in today's Iran, where the Safavid Empire once laid a 55-kilometer stretch of cobblestones in the sixteenth century to prevent salt pans[1] from forming—salt pans that could trap merchant convoys and their camels.

Five centuries later, the Lut Desert has changed very little. Stretches of those ancient cobblestones still wait for convoys. The sands rise and fall and rise and fall again as the winds whip up new ridges and flatten old dunes. As far as the eye can see, there is only sand: yellow, dry, and forlorn. The Lut is a great empty pan of heat, hotter than anywhere else on earth.

At the high margin of the hot sand sits a cluster of dome-shaped mud houses huddled tightly together and laced along narrow, snarled alleyways. From high up, the houses resemble groups of anthills. Some are punched higher toward the sky with a badgir, wind trap, an architectural feature that dates back two thousand years. Standing atop these anthill houses, the wind towers speed up the flow of air and act as natural air conditioners to provide some comfort from the brutal heat. This is the town of Kerman, tucked in the southeastern part of Iran. Its people, the Kermoonis, have learned to tame the fierceness of the desert sun by letting the wind that slices through the empty sands bring them cool air.

Life here is slow. Kermoonis are known for their warm hospitality and thick southern drawl. It is a place where people's lives are intertwined. Survival amidst nature's harsh and dry surroundings has bred a tightly linked community

---

[1] A salt pan is a flat expanse of ground covered with salt and other minerals, usually found in deserts.

*where interdependence simultaneously allows people to thrive
. . . and to suffocate.*

* * *

It is a late afternoon in September, and the scorching summer
heat has finally begun to abate. Slowly, the midday slumber
ends, as people rise from their afternoon naps to resume their
usual activities. In his mud house in the *Khaj-e Khezr*
neighborhood, Sadegh leans on floor cushions, sipping his tea.
He studies his daughter, Akhtar, slender and tentative as a fawn.
Her wavy black hair is pulled back into a single long braid, and
her thick, crescent-shaped eyebrows curve above her dark
almond eyes.

Akhtar kneels in front of him on the rug, reading the pages
of her schoolbooks.

Sadegh has never been to school. He can barely read or
write. He watches intently as his daughter effortlessly fills a page
with writing, her fingers tightly gripping a pencil. He imagines
what it must be like to sit in a classroom, to be initiated into the
secret world of letters, words, and poetry. Akhtar is at home in
this world.

But school is a luxury—a privilege—for a man. For a girl, it
is dangerous.

His family and neighbors speak out. They say it is wrong
and they warn Sadegh: "It's bad for a woman's mind! If women
learn to read and write they'll be writing notes inviting men to be
their boyfriends. Imagine how indecent that will be!"

Watching his daughter in the afternoon light, her head
bowed, nearly touching the book on the floor, he thinks how
sacred she seems. She reads while curled into the Muslim
position for prayer. He gazes at her with envy, yet with pride. He
has worked to give her what he never had.

When Akhtar finished her sixth year of school, he bought her
a wristwatch. Simple and small, with a clear face and a thin
brown strap. It is the first gift she ever received and she earned it

for doing well in school. Each morning, after her prayers, she slips it on as though she is wearing it for the very first time. She often polishes it with her headscarf. It is her badge of pride, hidden under her *chador*[2] with the schoolbooks she adores.

Akhtar is now in her tenth year of school. She is among only a handful of girls in town whose fathers have allowed their daughters to go beyond elementary school. Sadegh has watched her study nearly every day for ten years. But, the warnings ring more clearly now, like the cries of the watermelon vendor in the street coming closer and closer. He hears it as clearly as the call to prayer. Allah calls us to duty. Sadegh has a duty to Akhtar: to protect her beyond his life, to ensure that she is safe and financially secure. He also has defended her right to learn. Now he worries when they tell him, "She will become *torshideh,* sour, there aren't that many suitors in this small town. At her age, fewer and fewer."

"*Akhtaroo,*" says Sadegh, sitting crosslegged on a coarsely woven, maroon tribal rug. "Allah calls us to serve Him. It is our reward."

"Yes, Agha."

"You will understand, then?"

The sound of the watermelon vendor rises above the mud walls, rings through the courtyard and into the room.

Akhtar looks at her father closely. "If it is God's will," she says.

Sadegh lays a small photograph on the rug before Akhtar.

"You will bring this young man back to his faith. It's your religious duty to show this *yek-temcheh* orphan boy the clean life of a pious Muslim."

Akhtar glances at the photograph. She looks away. She can hear the voice of the watermelon seller fading away.

"How, Agha?"

"You will marry him."

"*Agha,* sir, please!"

---

[2] A chador is a loose robe worn like a cloak by some devout Muslims.

"You are ready to marry."

"You said I can study. You said you are proud of me, how well I do."

"You are sixteen. It is time to put a girl's life away."

She beseeches her father, "Please, Agha, let me finish my school!"

Sadegh slouches forward and pushes the photograph toward Akhtar. With his elbows resting on his knees, he starts to rotate his *tasbih,* a string of ninety-nine beads that Muslims use when praying, and murmurs *Allahu Akbar,* God is great. He gently passes each bead through the fingers of his right hand, trying to avoid Akhtar's tear-filled eyes. The small mud-walled room is quiet. Outside, a willow branch rustles against the courtyard stones, the water pump handle grinds, chickens cluck aimlessly, and the bell on a neighbor's goat rings. Akhtar turns back to her father.

"*Na azizam,* no my dear, there is no need for you to finish your school. You will have a husband to secure your future. Akhtar*oo,* this boy comes from a decent and honorable family, but they have not been devout. Now his parents are dead. This boy needs to have a home where a woman shines the love of Allah on him. It is your duty, Akhtar*oo.* Studying is not the duty of a woman. Ten years, that's more than enough schooling for you."

Akhtar's hand slips to the band of her wristwatch. She fights back tears. Swallowing hard, she asks, "*Chera,* Agha, *chera?* Why? Haven't I been a good student, Agha?"

Sadegh keeps his eyes cast down; voices run through his head. Education for a woman is a fanciful notion. His daughter must marry someone who can provide a good life for her. He cannot risk her financial security for the sake of education. Especially now, when Sadegh feels compelled to do good for a young man whose childhood was as difficult as his own. Allah has given him a decent life. He believes his deep faith has been rewarded. It is his duty to return God's generosity by helping another. God has brought the Karbassi boy, Reza, to him. The photograph rests on the rug in front of him, nearly touching the tip of his tasbih as it rotates through his fingers.

"Agha, Please let me finish." Akhtar begs, pushing back the photograph.

Sadegh simply shakes his head and twirls his tasbih until he comes to the last bead. It is tasseled, shaped like a tiny minaret, the tower from which the call to prayer is sounded. For a brief moment, he stops at that bead as though Akhtar might have a chance to dissuade him.

Chapter 3
Tasbih

Apart from physical features, I don't take after my mother's side of the family. I'm certainly not anything like my maternal grandfather, Sadegh. I don't mean that in an arrogant way. I say it wistfully.

I, like my mother, used to call my grandfather Agha, sir. From what I remember of him, I always stood a good distance away. He never talked to me directly. I was too young, and I was a girl. He was not the kind of grandfather who would pour out his affection to a female grandchild. He would never sit me down on his lap to tell me stories. A quiet, reserved man.

The family stories I tell you here were given to me by my mother. The lingering image I have of my Agha is of a religious man who rotated his tasbih.

A tasbih is a string of prayer beads, ninety-nine of them, constructed from a variety of materials—stones, olive seeds, ivory, amber, pearls, wood, even plastic. Observant Muslim men nearly always carry one. It helps them count the repetition of prayer verses, their lips forming words in praise of Allah in sync with each bead they rotate. As a verb, tasbih literally means "to travel swiftly"; as a noun, "duties." But the true meaning is really in the devotional context: *Sob'hana Allah,* will of God. And that's what Agha would have probably uttered, day in day out—*Sob'hana Allah*—holding his tasbih in his hand as he told my mother whom she must marry . . .

Kerman, Iran
1912

Approximately 120 kilometers west of Kerman is a mountain range with peaks more than 3,000 meters above sea level. The village of Lalehzaar, named for the carpets of tulips that blanket this lush and fertile region, lies at its foot. Here, clear mountain streams are surrounded by banks of mint and wild roses. Rows upon rows of apricot, plum, and walnut trees with thick, ancient trunks stand erect, like ancient elders, revered by those who harvest them. Pussy willow trees accent the mountainous trails where sheep roam freely, speckling the verdant background with white. It is an oasis in the desert. A place of refuge. And like its seared desert neighbor, this land holds several thousand years of history. It has been cultivated since the middle of the first millennium, when the people of this arid region learned to lead mountain water through qanats, a complex irrigation system that collects and transports water from the mountain. These underground conduits run from Lalehzaar to villages many kilometers away, bringing them the desert's most valuable resource: water. Kermoonis who make the trek to this village nearly always feel themselves reminded of Allah's greatness, of his ability to give and to take. The surrounding beauty seems to tell them that for those who live by His rules, there shall be rewards, and those who don't will suffer. Heaven and Hell. The blessed and the damned. The path is easily discernable, if you believe. While growing up, Sadegh often traveled the road that leads to Lalehzaar from Kerman. Each step helped shape his character. He believes there is only one path in life. And that is the will of Allah

* * *

The moon is still high, its faint light coming through the small, round window. Dawn is more than an hour away.

Jan-Bibi, a young mother—thirty-four years old, widowed at age twenty-five—kneels by her sleeping son, Sadegh. It is time for the 11-year-old to go to work. She watches his heart beat, listens to his soft breath. Who could disturb such angelic sleep?

"Sadegh . . . Sadegh joon," she coos. Her hand rests on his arm.

In the shadows, she can see his 14-year-old sister asleep close by. Jan-Bibi wipes her hands across her son's face and whispers, "Khodaya, Lord, protect this son of mine. He's all I have. *Allahu Akhbar*."

"Sadegh joon, wake up."

With a low moan, Sadegh begins to stir.

"*Azizam,* your uncle will leave soon. It's a travel day. You must get up."

Jan-Bibi strikes a match and lights a kerosene lamp. Sadegh steps over his sister's bedding, careful not to wake her. He heads toward the door of their one-room mud shack. Jan-Bibi stuffs a piece of bread in the pocket of Sadegh's tattered pants as he sleepily gropes around the doorstep for his shoes. Holding the kerosene lamp in one hand and pulling open the door with the other, she whispers a prayer in his ear before letting him out. All skin and bones, wearing patched clothes and cheap rubber shoes, Sadegh heads out into the alleyway. He can hear his mother's voice still reciting prayers when the wooden door of their room creaks shut.

It's hard for her to see him go into the dark alleyway, to work so that he can support her and her daughter. Some days the hope of her prayers cannot outweigh her sense of guilt. By custom, by community expectation, Jan-Bibi should have married Haj-Yazdi, her husband's brother. She should have become his second wife. She would have been able to live in his home—a comfortable life for herself and her children. There would have been plenty of food, decent clothing, and even some luxuries.

But the second wife must live and abide by the dictates of the first wife. Haj-Yazdi's first wife, Mahtala'at, is the queen of her fiefdom. She orders the servants around at her whim, and her generosity is further "proof" of her command. Jan-Bibi would be another household servant. She refused to marry Haj-Yazdi. Was it her youth or her grief, or simply pride?

For a young woman to live without a man shocked their small town. It was scandalous. It wasn't natural. It threatened their way of life. In the eyes of Allah, it would invite *fitna,* social chaos.

In a small town, where the houses face each other and away from the vast deserts, people sought to enforce customs in the only way they knew. They stared at the little family, whispered about them in the market. They offered advice that went unheeded. They added ridicule and insult to the pain she and her two children were already feeling.

Still, throughout the years there had been acts of kindness that helped them survive. Although she refused to marry him, Haj-Yazdi put a roof over their head, and from the time Sadegh was six he had been working for his uncle to earn money for his mother and sister. At first he would serve his uncle tea and run errands while Haj-Yazdi conducted his business. Now that he is older, Sadegh accompanies Haj-Yazdi to the lush hectares of land he owns near Mount Lalehzaar.

Jan-Bibi was willing to endure. She had made her choice. Her two young children, though, had no choice and still paid a price for her decision. She knew this in her heart, and it ached when she sent her little Sadegh to work each day.

Under a canopy of stars and the bright moon, Sadegh bumbles along, sleepwalking in an early morning dream. The sound of *azan* rises from a nearby mosque: a high-pitched, mournful melody calling to God, calling the community to rise for the first of their five daily prayers. *Alluah Akbar,* it wails. The azan calls Sadegh to duty. He hurries on to the compound of Haj-Yazdi.

His uncle's gunman is already standing at attention at the doorway, with his rifle and a horse harness in hand. Sadegh scoots next to him, stands at attention, and waits for his uncle. A few steps away, closer to the door, Mahtala'at waits patiently, draped in her white chador. She's a heavyset woman and is holding a small tray. Upon it there are a Koran, a mirror, and two bowls: one of water, the other of flour.

Mahtala'at has borne her husband eighteen children: nine have died. Of the nine who survived, six are girls and three are boys. Her husband's wealth has bestowed on her comfort and respect. She commands a platoon of *noono-rakhti* servants (those who are paid with food and clothing) and *kenez-gholams* (slaves Haj-Yazdi has bought in Bandar Abas). Mahtala'at spends her days visiting family members, who kneel and reverently kiss her hand. Beyond giving orders to her servants, Mahtala'at is expected to do little around the household. She rises early to do her duty only on the days her husband travels to Lalehzaar.

Sadegh yawns, wiping his sleepy eyes. Roosters announce the arrival of dawn. Sadegh can hear steps within. Finally, Haj-Yazdi steps out. He stops at the threshold and waits for Mahtala'at to raise the tray above his head. Carefully keeping her chador from slipping off her hair, Mahtala'at rises onto her tiptoes, stretching her arms so her husband can pass under the tray. Sadegh and the gunman stand, quietly watching.

Haj-Yazdi steps under the tray and through the doorway. Then he turns around to face the tray. He picks up the Koran and respectfully touches it to his forehead. Then he places his hand on the flour, an ever-so-light pat, almost as though he blesses the very bread the flour will make. (Later that morning, Mahtala'at will send a servant to give the flour to a family in need.) He then tilts his head down toward the tray to look in the small mirror, a reflection of the future's light and an assurance of life. Finally, as he mounts his horse, Mahtala'at, still clenching her white chador under her chin, murmurs *Van Ye Kad*, a traveler's prayer. She then splashes the bowl of water over her husband's departing heels. This final gesture is a pact with Allah: bring him home safely.

With Haj-Yazdi mounted on his finely saddled mare, Sadegh and the gunman, both on mules, fall into step behind him.

Sadegh listens to the sound of hooves as the three make their way through dirt alleyways and past mud houses.

Once they reach the open road, Haj-Yazdi motions his gunman to take the lead and to do his job: keep a keen eye out for bandits. The morning wears on. Heat waves shimmer along the horizon, and tamarisk bushes, scattered sporadically, spot the landscape. Sadegh trails behind, his reed-like body as skinny as the mule he rides. Sadegh studies his uncle's profile, how his body moves rhythmically up and down with the horse's steps, how his face is focused and intent on the road ahead, how he rarely looks to the side. A king on his throne. Nothing is said among the three.

Finally, at noon, Sadegh hears the sounds of rest.

"Whosshh," Haj-Yazdi says, pulling the harness of his horse.

Sadegh squints up at the sky and knows by the position of the sun that it is time for the noon *namaz,* the second daily prayer. Taking the harness from his uncle, Sadegh helps him dismount.

"Pesar, boy, take some of God's dirt." Haj-Yazdi instructs Sadegh. Like a teacher testing his student, he asks, "What did I tell you about this dirt?"

Haj-Yazdi's father was born a Zoroastrian but was forced to convert to Islam. Converting was a matter of survival, of having bread to eat. There were consequences—most often fatal—for those who refused to convert. Haj-Yazdi's father gave up his beliefs so that his family could live. He had no other choice. When it came to Haj-Yazdi, fear became transformed into zeal. A father's desperation became his son's strict devotion.

Sadegh bows his head in respect and recites, "The Prophet Muhammad has instructed us that in the absence of water we are allowed to cleanse ourselves with God's earth."

Haj-Yazdi grunts, displeased that his nephew has forgotten the main point of his question. "And what does the prophet call this in the Koran?"

"It's called *Tayammum*, sir," he says. Then, to please his uncle, he adds, "And the prophet also instructs us that any rock along such a desert road suffices for *sang-e namaz,* prayer stone."

"*Kho'b, kho'b.* Okay, okay. Don't waste any more time," Haj-Yazdi says to both the gunman and Sadegh.

Sadegh and the gunman take their positions a few steps behind Haj-Yazdi, all three facing west toward Mecca, the house of Allah. The three pick up dirt and pat it on the palms of their hands. They then bring their palms to their foreheads and down their faces before they stroke their hands against each other. Standing with his companions in the middle of the desolate and barren landscape, Sadegh, a foot shorter than either the gunman or his uncle, opens his palms toward the sky in prayer. Looking to the heavens with his eyes closed and the ochre furnace of the Lut Desert burning around him, he recites the verses of noon namaz.

Kerman
1949

The room remains still. The voice of the watermelon seller returns as he winds his mule-drawn cart back through the streets, heading for home. His call is melodic and rhythmic, the same call, day in and day out, like his father and the fathers before him.

"*Sob'hana Allah,* Will of God." Sadegh continues to murmur. Akhtar listens. She is looking at her father's face—the image of a hardworking religious man—while his dry, laborer's hands rotate the tasbih beads, his lips reciting the praises of Allah. Sadegh's eyes are closed. Akhtar waits, as if time has stopped, waiting for his fingers to reach the last bead.

Finally, her father speaks. "What would Allah want me to do? What would people say? Akhtaroo, I will not be able to hold my head high in this town if you were to continue your schooling."

Sadegh wanted to give his beautiful daughter everything. But, a father cannot—he must follow the wisdom of the elders, the will of God. A father must raise his daughter under the strict code of female honor. His daughter has observed *hijab,* preserving her womanly dignity beneath the veil she has worn since she was nine. Knowing that his daughter was raised in a decent Muslim family allows Sadegh to walk tall in Kerman.

"*Baleh,* yes, Agha," she says keeping her gaze on the rich burgundy and dark blue rug she is kneeling on. Searching for something to say, her eyes dart across the carpet's design of stylized camel footprints surrounded by a geometric border of predictably symmetrical lines. Shapes that entrap. Resting her eyes on a worn-out edge of the carpet, Akhtar concedes that there is no other option and stops her futile attempt to change her father's mind. What can she say to a man who has only known one road in life? Who counts his blessings and never asks for more than what God has already given him? Whose own marriage to Tayebeh, a first cousin, Haj-Yazdi's second youngest daughter, was strictly governed by tradition and custom. What can Akhtar say or do?

"The boy is working in Tehran right now. He will come in the spring, but we will register your marriage before then," her father says. "Now please, go get me some tea."

He slides the small photograph toward her.

Akhtar cannot look up. She feels the thick knot in her stomach rising into her chest. She takes the three-by-five photograph from the rug and lifts herself up to bring him tea. She keeps her head down as she ducks through the low rounded doorway into the courtyard.

Nothing can ever be the same

Akhtar slips into rubber sandals. Her feet scrape across the dusty tiles. She crosses the courtyard and passes the opening where, down six steps, there is a cool, pungent room where they keep chickens. She stops a moment and looks down into the dark space. Some days she goes down into that space to gather freshly laid eggs; on other days she retrieves a chicken to be slaughtered for the midday meal. Either way, one life is sacrificed. It's just a matter of timing.

At the foot of the well, pumping the metal handle to fill the bucket of dirty laundry at her feet, Akhtar sees their servant, Kobra. Long before Akhtar was born, Kobra came to live with the family. When Tayebeh married Sadegh, Haj-Yazdi sent one of his youngest servants, Kobra, to help Tayebeh and Sadegh in their new household. Kobra had been orphaned as a young child and had grown up in Haj-Yazdi's household. She's blind in one eye, the pupil muddy with a bluish-purple vein across it.

Kobra calls out to her.

Akhtar sees her as if for the first time. Kobra's pudgy figure is wrapped at the waist with a chador, her right arm slamming the metal pump handle, sweat beading on her brow. Then Kobra squats, her elbows against her thighs, as she scrubs, beats, and kneads dirty clothes. Time and time again. A lifetime.

Akhtar continues moving across the courtyard toward two connecting rooms. Meals are prepared here. It is Akhtar's most cherished part of the house, a space she often shares with her grandmother, Jan-Bibi. It is the place she eagerly runs to when she has something fun to share with her grandmother. But at this moment, she walks toward it with a sense of doom, realizing that soon her life in this house—familiar and loving—will come to an end. She takes a peek at the photograph in her hand and pushes her feet to step forward. She enters the cooking area, its walls black with soot from the two stoves where her grandmother often stands and stirs large cooking pots over an open flame. There is also a *tanoor,* a cavernous stone hearth where bread is baked. Once each week, a middle-aged woman, their neighborhood breadmaker, visits their house. She comes wrapped in her chador and spends the day kneading dough and slapping the flattened circles against the inside walls of the stove's hot cavity, inside the tanoor. On those days, Akhtar sits next to her grandmother and wraps the freshly made bread bundles into thick cloths that they use to keep the bread fresh until the baker woman's next visit.

Akhtar steps out of the sun and into the cooking rooms, breathing in the scents of mint, tarragon, cumin, and turmeric—the smells of her home. Kept among the stacks of pots and pans there are large tins of animal fat, burlap sacks of rice, and bottles of dried herbs. She looks to the tanoor. Her grandmother is not there. Nor is she stirring any of the large pots over the open fire. Akhtar suddenly feels lost.

"What is it *bacheh,* child?" The voice comes out of the dusty corner.

At the foot of the sundry room, sitting on an old, worn-out rug peeling onions, is her grandmother. Akhtar stands there for a while, long enough that Jan-Bibi asks again, "Tell me what's happened to you girl! *Chi Shodeh?*"

Akhtar kneels on the worn carpet next to her 65-year-old grandmother. Jan-Bibi puts down the onion and wipes her watery eyes with her chador.

"Where is my happy girl? *Begoo,* tell me—is it school?"

Akhtar shows her grandmother the photograph of the boy. Tears begin to roll down her cheeks again. "Agha wants me to marry this man."

Jan-Bibi takes the photograph and brings it closer to her dimmed eyes. The young man in the photograph wears a suit and a tie, his hair is sleek. She stares at the photograph for what seems a long time.

"He's a modern type, a city man," she says.

Akhtar nods.

"Not a son of a merchant or a mullah," Jan-Bibi adds. Akhtar knows this.

The two look at the photograph. There is an uneasy silence as each woman searches for a word to express her feelings. Old and weathered, Jan-Bibi looks at the photograph from a perspective of age: restrained, pragmatic, and weary. Akhtar, young and naive, stares at it with stupefied anticipation. Each wants to say something, but the words refuse to be spoken.

A rooster pokes its head into the doorway, its red crown flopping to one side.

"Ai! Away!" Jan-Bibi cries out. The rooster cocks its head, eyes flashing, unmoved. "Ai!" she says again, with force. The rooster retreats.

Jan-Bibi returns her gaze to her granddaughter, who sits in front of her. She struggles to say something comforting. But what can she say? Women must marry. Life brings pain. Still, Akhtar is her favorite. If only a grandmother could soothe her anxiety with just words.

After gazing at the photograph for a long time, she begins. "He looks *najib,* decent. His eyes show a young man who has no ill intentions."

Akhtar's eyes find the eyes of her grandmother. There are so many questions Akhtar wants to ask her grandmother. Jan-Bibi tries to fill her own gaze with all that she hopes for the granddaughter who has brought her such joy. Is there a moment when all can be said in one look?

She knows her granddaughter has no choice. She has learned that there are some things in life that are simply one's fate. She has accepted it as God's will. This path, she believes, is Akhtar's.

Breathing in deeply, Jan-Bibi murmurs a prayer. "*B'Omid Khoda.* With the hope of God, child." Jan-Bibi caresses Akhtar's cheek. "*B'Omid Khoda.*"

Gently, Akhtar takes the photograph from her and gets up to take tea to her father.

Within two weeks the paperwork is signed. Akhtar is married to the photograph. Without meeting the boy, she has signed her marriage papers in Kerman while the boy in the photograph—Reza Karbassi—has signed the marriage papers in Tehran. She will wait for the marriage ceremony in the spring.

Every day seems the same as before, but everything has changed. Akhtar continues going to school, with Sadegh's permission. But she knows school will end. Each day school seems like a precious luxury, and each night is spent with the photograph.

Akhtar leans her head on a pillow in her room and imagines what it will be like to meet her husband. She studies his face in the photograph. Is he najib? Will he be kind? Will he understand how much she loves school and perhaps let her continue? She talks to him through the photograph. Sometimes she cries.

Above Akhtar's bed is a small *tagh-cheh,* a shelf carved into the mud wall. Each night, before she puts out the kerosene lamp, Akhtar puts Reza's photograph in the tagh-cheh. She keeps everything she owns there: a prayer satchel, her watch, and now her photograph husband.

Fall and winter pass. The family waits until Reza is able to travel to Kerman for their *aroosi*—the wedding celebration, the night when the entire family will gather for a feast.

The man in Akhtar's photograph arrives in Kerman in spring of 1950. He is her husband and she is his wife—the papers are all signed, but they have not met. His only chance to appraise his wife has been through Ohadi, the old Kermani friend who has served as the intermediary with Sadegh. Ohadi has told him that Akhtar is ideal for Reza—she is literate, open-minded enough for the young bureaucrat's life in Tehran, but traditional enough to obey him.

Reza Karbassi steps off the bus in Kerman in early March, met only by the sweet breeze of spring. Throughout the village, Kermoonis are busy preparing for *Noruz,* the arrival of the Persian new year. The dust of the old year must be driven away. Reza can see carpets hung outside, servants beating away the dust with broom handles.

He sees a man with a brown paper bag. Air holes punched through its sides release a merry chirping sound: baby chicks for the New Year—just as when he was a boy in Kerman. He sees an old man kneeling by the corner of a blanket, where he sells goldfish from a bucket and wheat sprouts from a plate for the New Year tradition of *Haft Sīn,* the setting upon which families lay symbolic items for the coming of the new year. Reza remembers how he and his siblings used to help their mother set the items that would go on *Haft Sīn.* Seven of them must, according to tradition, begin with the Farsi letter "s": *Seeb* (apple), *samanu* (wheat germ pudding), *seer* (garlic), *senjed* (bohemian dates), *sekeh* (coins), *somaq* (sumac), and, of course, *sabzeh* (sprouts). Each year, his mother would repeat the symbolic meaning of each … *sabzeh for rebirth*, rings in Reza's ear.

As Reza eagerly steps along the dirt alleyway in his freshly polished shoes, thoughts of his childhood in this town seem something from a distant past. His brand new suit gives him a feeling of importance as he walks confidently toward the Khaje-Khezr neighborhood. But something stops his stride.

"Pass it here, pass it here," he hears. Through a half-opened door, Reza sees two boys wearing rubber slippers playing soccer. For a moment Reza thinks it is Javad, his younger brother, calling for the ball as Reza dribbles around the walnut tree in their courtyard. Reza stops to see more. He imagines his mother at the head of the courtyard, instructing a servant to deliver a basket of food to a convalescing neighbor. He seems to see his father sitting crosslegged on a rug, laughing heartily with fellow Kermani merchants; his two inseparable sisters are huddled together, learning to sew. Reza stiffens with anguish. A brokenhearted boy lurks within. Then a discreet cough comes from within the compound. He has lingered too long, gazing at strangers.

Reza moves on. The dirt and dust of the alleyway have already begun to dull his polished shoes. His brand new suit with the skinny tie is crisp and fresh. He is an emblem of the new Iran. And, he realizes, he is a stranger in Kerman. Even though he is the grandson of Abolghassem, even though he is a Karbassi. He takes a deep breath. The Kermoonis do not know him—they don't know, he reminds himself, that he is at the center of the new Iran. That makes him feel important as he walks the narrow dirt path toward Khaje-Khezr.

Turning a corner, he meets two women in black chadors who are gripping the ends of the long, dark fabric under their chins. They study Reza as he passes. He is still a stranger. Reza feels their eyes on him long past the alleyway's bend—Kerman's small-town surveillance. Their houses are turned inward, their eyes toward each other. He feels deeply uneasy. He wishes he were in a taxi among the honking horns on the broad modern streets of Tehran.

Meanwhile, inside Akhtar's house, they have all been busy since dawn preparing the house for the arrival of Reza, their guest. Is he a guest? Or is he family? It has been decided that he will be received in the guestroom—the best room in the house.

Right after their morning prayers, Akhtar, along with her mother, grandmother, and Kobra, have pulled the rugs out from the guestroom and beat them with brooms, each strike sending winter dust wafting through the clean morning air. They have swept the courtyard, bending again and again over the *hozcheh* to fill pails of water, which they splash across the courtyard tiles. By late morning the house is thoroughly cleaned, and a large teapot is brewing atop the samovar.

Reza arrives at the house with a thin layer of dust over his shoes, his hair still carefully combed and shiny. At the old wooden door of Sadegh's house, he hesitates and looks from side to side. He is nervous, but his duty lies behind the old door in front of him: his duty to his ancestors to sire a family.

Even the door carefully prescribes the duties of men and women. There are two door knockers: one for males, the other for females. The first, made with heavier metal, gives a deeper sound that warns the family that a male visitor waits outside the door, allowing the women inside to gather their chadors over their heads, covering themselves so that their chastity and family honor are preserved. The presence of men other than their *mahram*—husbands, fathers, brothers, or sons—requires that they appear modest, their hair concealed, their female shapes hidden. Only in the presence of their mahram can they reveal themselves, though still only a little. Reza reaches for the male knocker, a lion's head.

He raps several times, bringing the Farivarmeheen household to attention. Sadegh heads into the guestroom. Tayebeh and Jan-Bibi follow, Akhtar slips behind a wall to hide, and Kobra makes her way to the door, pulling her chador over her hair and holding its ends under her chin.

The old wooden door creaks open.

"*Salam-o Aleykom,*" Reza says to Kobra, whose nose is about the only thing visible.

"*Aleykom-o salam,*" Kobra responds, mirroring the greeting, and politely motions him to enter. Reza steps down and waits for her to close the door.

Kobra then ushers him to the guestroom, the doors of which have been opened for their guest. Smelling sweetly of bakhlava, pistachios, and dried fruit, the room is welcoming. An intricately designed floral rug is spread across the floor, and large *poshti* floor cushions rest side by side along the walls for guests to lean on. An ornately shaped water pipe rests in one corner. Although Sadegh himself does not smoke, he does occasionally prepare the tall glass water pipe for his guests.

Reza lowers his head to pass under the archway into the guestroom, keeping it tipped down when he sees Sadegh standing. He notices Tayebeh and Jan-Bibi standing next to each other a few feet behind Sadegh, both hidden under their chadors, their eyes fixed on the carpet.

"Aghay-e Karbassi." Sadegh addresses Reza formally by calling him "sir" in addition to his surname, even though this young man has now been his son-in-law for nearly six months. "Please sit down." He motions Reza to take a seat along one of the larger cushions, those reserved for important guests. Located farthest from the doorway, it's the spot called "top of the room," offered only to those most elevated in status.

"*Ghorban shoma,*" Reza responds ceremonially, bowing deeply in gratitude to Sadegh and the two women before taking his seat.

It is impolite for a man to face a woman directly, and Reza sits with his head turned away from the two women. He keeps his eyes discreetly focused on Sadegh, who sits on a floor cushion directly in front of him.

Tayebeh and Jan-Bibi sit quietly, allowing Sadegh to talk with Akhtar's husband. They listen and observe as though they were not present, but they are in fact very alert. Tucked behind their chadors, the two women are intensely curious about the Karbassi boy.

They have heard the rumors. In a small town like Kerman, they have heard of his family's past misfortunes. For months the gossip around their neighborhood has focused on why the Farviarmeheen family would give their daughter to the Karbassi boy.

The Karbassi family has fallen on hard times. Most people believe that the family's fate is God's punishment for lack of piety. "This is the price they've paid for not being devout," they say knowingly. Others think differently. Some say it was the family's wealth that beckoned the evil eye; in a time when many Kermoonis had no bread to eat, the Karbassi house was full—an overstuffed storehouse, filled to the brim with its liquor and opium. No wonder the boy fled to Tehran. And what is Tehran after all but "the bastion of impious lives?"

Now he is here in their home, with his fancy suit and tie and neatly shaven. Does he think he is better than other Kermoonis? And they say that he is not devout. Tayebeh and Jan-Bibi wonder why Sadegh has chosen this city boy for Akhtar.

Does Sadegh see something of himself in Reza? Each lost his father when he was young. Each became the head of the family without the seasoning of time or the guidance of an elder. Sadegh found strength in God and in prayer. He cannot will faith onto the young man. But he can offer his daughter, who will guide Reza back to God. Through this union, he can rejoice and serve Allah.

Tayebeh and Jan-Bibi listen to the polite, formal talk between father and son-in-law. Sadegh does not probe Reza; he does not seek proof that Reza will be a good husband. It is understood that each man will do his duty.

Sadegh is not a literate man, but he knows that the world is changing. The orchards and fields of Kerman represent the old way. Here is a young man who must understand the ways of the new Iran. The young man works for the Shah in the Iranian oil company. He wears the white shirt and skinny tie. This must be the future that Sadegh can never know. Still, Sadegh is sure that this young man will guide Akhtar safely into the future . . . with God's will.

Akhtar waits hidden behind a wall outside the guestroom. She listens to the men's conversation. She secretly tries to glance inside, but Reza sits too far into the corner for her to see him. For the first time, she hears her photograph speak. The meanings of the words are bland: mundane formality. She strains to hear the voice, the sounds of the words. These are the sounds she will hear for a lifetime. Her heart pounds inside her chest. She asks herself for the millionth time, do the words come from the voice of a kind man?

When Sadegh calls Akhtar, it will be the signal for her to
bring tea. Akhtar is poised by the samovar. She doesn't know if
she is soaked from the steam of the samovar or the sweat of fear.

Jan-Bibi comes to check on her. She strokes Akhtar's long
braid, then takes her nervous hands and squeezes them gently.
With her old hands, Jan-Bibi tries to reassure her granddaughter,
to tell her what she is about to go through is all part of life's
cycle, natural and welcome. Yet Akhtar's eyes flash with worry.
Life's path leads to one's destiny, this becomes clear when you
look back in old age, Akhtar thinks. But looking ahead there is
no path, only her heart thrown into the wind.

"Give me the tray, Akhtar joon," Jan-Bibi says to her.

Akhtar stands dead still, staring at the samovar. Jan-Bibi
takes the teapot from atop the charcoal-burning samovar and
pours dark tea into three thin, short glasses, filling them halfway.
The aroma of tea fills the air.

"Akhtar joon, this is life," Jan-Bibi says. "We have to live
with the path that we are given." Jan-Bibi fills the fragile beakers
to the top with hot water from the samovar's spout, "This
Karbassi boy is now your husband. You have to go and build a
life with him."

Akhtar nods and looks enviously into the eyes of an old
woman who shared her life with a man only briefly. Jan-Bibi
didn't marry her brother-in-law after her husband died, ignoring
duty and custom. She made her own decision. *Was I asked what
I want?* Akhtar thinks.

"Your path is to follow him wherever he goes."

Akhtar remains frozen in place. Jan-Bibi places the three
beakers of tea on the tray beside a silver bowl filled with sugar
cubes and dates.

"*Bacheh,* child, it's rude to keep our guest waiting. Go. Take
this tray. Take this tray and make the best with what God gives
you in life. Go."

"*Chashm,*" an obedient yes, she says to Jan-Bibi. "*Chashm.*"

Jan-Bibi smoothes Akhtar's ankle-length skirt and pinches her cheeks to enliven her complexion. Slipping on a flowered blue headscarf, Akhtar takes the tray from her grandmother and nervously heads toward the guestroom.

With open palms toward heaven, Jan-Bibi murmurs a verse from the Koran, the verse of *Van Ye Kad,* the one that asks Allah to protect one's journey. She ends her prayer with a gentle blow, like putting out a candle, sending the prayer on its way to follow her granddaughter's steps.

Akhtar halts at the threshold to the guestroom. Here are the street shoes of the household. One pair is black, freshly polished—the shoes of her husband. Swallowing hard, she enters the room. Reza jumps to his feet in respect. He stutters a muffled greeting, keeping his eyes down. He dare not look directly at his wife in front of her father. Akhtar, too, keeps her eyes fixed on the tea tray. Shyness and propriety keep their eyes apart.

Akhtar steals a glance, capturing all she can in the forbidden sweep of her eyes. His jet-black hair is combed neatly back and shines brightly of paraffin. He is thin and tall, dressed in a striped suit, a white shirt, and a black tie.

Reza catches only the strands of thick hair peeking from under her scarf. She is biting her lip. Both stand awkwardly, unsure of what to do, their eyes avoiding one another. A moment passes before Sadegh urges Reza to sit back down on the rug and tells Akhtar to serve the tea. Bending courteously forward, with her family looking on, she offers her husband *chai.* With one hand Reza takes a beaker and with the other a syrupy fresh date from Akhtar's waiting hands.

In these few seconds, Sadegh has completed his duty as a father, while Akhtar and Reza have begun their long life together.

Narragansett
2005

"You may pour my chai," Reza says, struggling to seat himself at the kitchen table.

Lifting the teapot from the stove, Akhtar pours the amber colored tea into two glass beakers. She brings one of the beakers close to her nose. The rising steam caresses her wrinkled face, and she breathes in the familiar aroma of tea leaves laced with the subtle scent of pussy-willow flowers. The fragrance takes her back to Kerman, where the hot drink is a delicacy. When she was a child, Sadegh once took her to Lalehzaar, the same trek he had made decades before with Haj-Yazdi. There she got to witness the marriage of this leaf and the wildflower. In Lalehzaar, where pussy-willow trees thrive along icy-cold mountain rivers, Akhtar watched local village women, dressed in headscarves and full-length, billowing clothing in florid colors, collecting the fuzzy little catkins. The water lapped along stony river banks as the squatting women spread the soft furry tips of the branches—tiny buds just shy of being scentless—upon cotton sheets. Kerman's powerful sun then blended the delicate scent of pussy willows with the strong tea leaves. It was if one's weakness strengthened the other.

"What's the occasion? Are we expecting guests this morning?" Reza asks with a jab of cynicism. Akhtar brews this tea only for guests, and there haven't been many in recent memory. Even their children rarely visit.

Akhtar looks over at the tea canister sitting atop the yellow Formica counter. Her father sent this batch of tea to her more then two decades ago. While he was still alive, he'd send her small packages from Kerman every so often. Tea along with little bags of spice—dried dill, tarragon, and cumin—bundled together in a box that was covered with his botched, childish handwriting. He usually included a short letter for her, mere sentences that he had managed to learn to spell out. One sentence always said, *Moman'at salam miresaneh,* your mother says hello. Thin words from her mother, which made the distance far greater than the miles of oceans and deserts that separated them. *"Salam miresaneh."* What else could an illiterate old woman send across the oceans of distance?

Akhtar clears her throat to say something, but pauses. She wants to tell him that yes, she *has* been frugal in using this tea. But why? Why *did* she keep this tea stashed for more than twenty years? Treasured it, perhaps; denied it, certainly. The reason escapes her. All she knows now is that it's time for it to brew. Liberally. Thinking *this keeps the promise of home within reach* as she breathes in the tea's flowery essence, she feels the anticipation of going home.

"I've kept it far longer than I should have," she says softly to Reza after a while, keeping her eyes straight down at her tea. "There's no reason to keep it anymore. Throwing things away in the garage has made me realize that our lives have slipped away . . . right before our very eyes." Then, lifting her eyes to meet Reza's, she adds, "What have *we* been waiting for, Karbassi? It passed us . . . our lives . . . it slipped right past . . . Like shreds of old cloth we are now . . . bare threads and holes, that's all we are . . ." Her voice quivers and trails off. She looks at a tea leaf floating in her glass, like a drifter away from home. Reza doesn't say anything. After a pause, she continues, "We've been on hold here for so long, we've forgotten who we are. We're neither here nor there. We're somewhere in between, suspended, lost." She wonders if going through their stuff in the garage has left her rattled and confused. She rarely talks this way, like she's the one in charge. She surprises herself. "It's time we drank it, Karbassi," she says with finality. Reza reaches for the piping hot beaker before him. His hands jitter, rattling the beaker against the saucer. Its nervous chatter is his response. For a while they eat her homemade bread as they usually do: without conversation. Akhtar can hear Reza's dentures clicking with each bite he takes. A lawn mower revs its engine and breaks the early morning peace. She asks herself, *How did we even end up here? Being so isolated, so far away. Of all places, in this small town?* Coming to America was one thing, but moving to Narragansett . . .

* * *

There were lots of boxes to be filled up. Boxes seemed to be part of every turn in their lives. This time they were in their New York City apartment, and each filled box gave Akhtar a secret sense of pleasure. She was counting down the days until they would return to Iran. It was 1975, near the end of Reza's four-year post in New York. Soon they would ship their lives back home.

Reza came home from his Manhattan office that evening. He sat at the oval kitchen table that later followed them to Narragansett. Reza sounded like he was still at the office— barking orders, delivering his words as if he were dictating to a secretary.

"Not all of us will go," he said, "Khanom, you will stay here—with the children—until they get their college degrees."

Akhtar's heart sank. Her youngest was only thirteen—five years from even starting college.

"I will go to Tehran," Reza continued. "Keyhan will come after he graduates."

The family will be on two continents.

And her parents? What about them? Sadegh and Tayebeh were in their seventies. She hadn't seen them for three years. They were old and getting older. How much time could they have? It would take at least seven years for all three children to earn college degrees.

"American education—it's the best in the world," Reza said, as he always did. "Good education, better life."

Akhtar felt as though her prison term was suddenly extended. At the very moment she was starting to feel free, years were added to her term.

But Akhtar never told Reza any of her objections—not that Reza would have listened. Reza was right, she thought.

Education is the most valuable investment. Staying in the United States seems a small price to pay for something so valuable. And it was for her children. For them, she was willing to do anything.

In the next few days, Reza charted their life's new course. He made the arrangements without consulting Akhtar. His priority was to find a place where, his family would be safe in his absence. New York City was not safe, not for his wife and children.

Reza relied on a senior American colleague at NIOC for advice. Allen, with his silver hair and blue eyes, had befriended Reza when he first arrived in America. Allen was a mentor, guide, and friend. In Reza's eyes, Allen could do no wrong.

"Rhode Island is the place—little Rhody—idyllic— wholesome as apple pie," Allen said.

Wholesome as apple pie? That meant nothing to Reza. He wanted a place for his family to live, not dessert.

"It's safe, Reza," Allen assured him. "Narragansett—in Rhode Island."

That's all Reza needed to hear. It took him longer to learn to pronounce the town's name than to buy the house. Soon the oval kitchen table was moved from New York to Narragansett.

* * *

"Uhum," Reza repeats several times. "Are you going to pour some more tea?" indicating with his eyes the empty beaker before him, "What's gotten into you this morning? Too much dust in that garage gotten into your tiny brain?"

Akhtar does not respond. She rises from her seat to get her husband his tea. As she tips the teapot, her gaze falls from the beaker in front of Reza to the chipped veneered cabinets, and then to the worn-out linoleum floor.

"Enough!" Reza barks as the tea nears the rim.

Akhtar stops. She is lost in her thoughts.

She looks down at the oval kitchen table. It was only supposed to be there for seven years. Now, thirty-three years later, there it is in exactly the same spot, battered, but otherwise, exactly the same.

* * *

Reza bought the oval kitchen table right away when they arrived in New York in 1971. Akhtar would have been fine without one. They could have spread a cloth on the ground and eaten on the floor as she did as a child in Kerman. After all, that's how most traditional Iranian families ate, and their apartment had wall-to-wall carpeting. But Reza balked at such a proposition. He considered sitting on the ground backwards, something only uneducated religious families would do—not, he stressed, someone like him.

"I have studied in London. I work for NIOC in America— the greatest country on earth. Eating on the ground is for the uncivilized, the uneducated, the religious people with their backward ways," Reza would say. A table moved Reza up in the world. It was a sign of modernity. A sign that he was Westernized.

The table had four matching chairs. Two were smashed by Reza in his fits of anger. Akhtar quietly replaced the chairs with cheaper versions from a second-hand shop. She didn't ask Reza for money, paying for it instead with what she had earned baking bread—kneading the dough on the very same oval table.

* * *

Akhtar sits down and once again inhales the rising steam of her tea. Reza continues to struggle with his glass. Unable to raise it steadily to his mouth, he dips his head down toward the beaker— bowing to his tea—and taking a cautious sip.

Akhtar watches him bow. She thinks of the photo in the garage, of Reza bowing to the Shah. But now his life is dominated by a new master: Parkinson's disease.

They finish their breakfast in silence. A shaft of morning light finally shines through the narrow window. Akhtar continues to dwell on how it was that they ended up here. A lawnmower still purrs across the neighbor's green grass. The sound reminds her of the very first glimpse she had of America. It was a vibrant colored photograph of a green California lawn. Akhtar used to stare at it for hours, captivated. She'd examine every detail, marveling at the beauty and mystery of this faraway place. In the picture, her uncle and his family look so happy, standing in the sun on grass greener than she had ever seen before. With their happy smiles, they look as if they are ready to tell you a great secret. The photograph was taken in her uncle's backyard, an uncle the family called Khan Daee, Great Uncle. He was her mother's brother, Haj-Yazdi's youngest son. The story of how he ended up in America was told back home with such great pride that Akhtar used to think of it as a fairy tale. She received the photograph in the mail when she and Reza first moved to Tehran. Khan Daee had sent the same photograph to everyone in the family.

In the photograph, Khan Daee is sitting straight-backed in a lawn chair. Sitting next to him is his wife, Nosrat, and standing behind them are their three sons and their American brides, primly dressed. Blonde hair, all three. His sons, Akhtar's cousins, appear to be in their twenties. All eight of them are wearing wide grins, probably saying "cheese."

Khan Daee sent the photograph to impress everyone in the family, and it worked. Akhtar was mesmerized by it. Relatives talked about his determination and his skill at amassing what surely must be a great fortune. Akhtar had heard the story of her uncle many times—how he had always dreamed of going to America even though he grew up in Kerman, a town that few ever left. His own father, the great landowner Haj-Yazdi, only traveled to Lalehzaar by horse with a gunman riding in front and

Sadegh following on a donkey. That was as far as anyone had traveled in those days.

Looking at the photograph in Tehran, Akhtar would see the white border around the picture as a boundary—she couldn't cross into the picture. How did Khan Daee mange to cross the boundary into America?

Akhtar knows that her uncle not only crossed the borders; he assimilated into the fabric of this huge, mixed-up country. Though he visited Iran often, Khan Daee never returned to his roots. He died on his new country's soil, his grandchildren fully American, their connections to Iran all but lost. The story of Khan Daee's life was reflected in that photograph taken in his sunny backyard in California: a man who has made it, an image of envy for all the relatives he left back home. Did Khan Daee accept America because America accepted him? Was it because he arrived there at a time when Iranians didn't carry the burdens of the Revolution and the hostage crisis? Akhtar wonders.

Khan Daee and Nosrat once paid the Karbassis a visit in New York City—an honor for Akhtar and Reza. Finally, here was the man she had heard about all her life, her uncle. Akhtar still remembers the story he told them during that visit.

* * *

When I was young, I had the privilege of going to school. My father, Haj-Yazdi—with all his land and money—wanted me to have the formal education he never had. Who could go to school in those days—before the Shah, before Iranians controlled the oil? What was a son for in those days but to work for the father, to make money for the family? My father decided to educate me. A luxury. I'm sure he calculated that with my education I would join him and build-up the business with all my new knowledge. He saw Kerman from atop of his great horse. How could he know that I could see the world through my books?

Akhtar, your father worked under my father—hard work, riding to Lalehzaar with a gunman, saying his prayers in the dust under the blazing desert sun. I was in a schoolhouse with my nose in a book, reciting lessons while he traveled that long, dusty road. I was a rich man's son with time to think for myself.

Khan Daee paused. He looked at Akhtar as if asking for forgiveness. Akhtar filled his cup with tea. He didn't hear her sigh.

I was fifteen when I told my father: I want to go to America.

Was he angry? No, he was furious! I had insulted him. The school had filled me with nonsense, silly dreams that no boy of his should have. I had become a wild horse and must be tamed. He had his patriarchal rights, so he knew that his commands would be followed.

But, my father was wrong.

I told one of my brothers that I was running away to Tehran and from there I'd make it to America. I snuck off in the dead of night with one of my father's mules. It was 1911.

Years later, I heard that when my father was informed by one of our servants that I had left, he remained calm. He thought I wouldn't last more than a few days in that bustling city of Tehran. He was wrong again.

It took years, but I eventually made it to the United States and settled in Carmel, California, a town on the Monterey Peninsula famous for its poets, painters, and writers.

I stumbled onto Carmel by accident—like most immigrants with no plan. But I liked Carmel by the Pacific Ocean. I'm not a poet or painter, so what could I do?

My father understood land. He wanted me to be a landowner. So, I started a construction business and began to buy land as soon as I could. It was land my father never could have dreamed of: not land for tulips and orchards and dates, but little lots of land for houses. I bought land, built houses and sold them . . . and I thrived. And here I am today.

Khan Daee paused to savor a Sair date from Kerman—a treat in New York that Akhtar had saved for a special occasion. Khan Daee sipped his tea and continued.

Reza, you are a Karbassi—you know the stories of your family. But did you know that I met your grandfather, Abolghassem? Yes, it hardly seems true—but it is. I was on the road between Kerman and Tehran. The thrill of running away from home was rapidly fading. I had seen no one for miles. I was hot, hungry, and tired.

I saw him up ahead—a big man with a big beard. Was he a bandit? Why was he traveling alone? Should I hide? But I was too tired to do anything.

He drew closer. We stopped, greeted each other, and dismounted. He invited me to share a piece of bread. I had nothing to offer him—I had forgotten to pack food for my trip. I bowed deeply in gratitude.

We sat down together to enjoy his bread. When I found out who he was, I was thrilled. He was famous in Kerman. He told me proudly that he was coming back from prison in Shiraz. They put me in jail for loving Persia, he told me. Then he quoted a simple line from one of Iran's greatest poets, Ferdowsi. He said, "If every one of us dies one by one, it is better than giving our country to the enemy."

He asked me where I was going. I was excited and told him that I was going to America.

I should have kept my mouth shut.

His great bushy eyebrows furrowed and he looked at me with a strange combination of pity and disdain.

He snatched his bread from my hand, got up, and left.

* * *

And now, my dear Reza, what would the great Abolghassem say about us? Living in this foreign country?

Chapter 4
Shimr

I've heard so many stories of my great-grandfather Abolghassem that I almost feel I've met the man myself. I have a framed daguerreotype of him sitting on my children's piano in our suburban American home. In this faded photograph, one of the oldest relics of my family's past, Abolghassem wears a silk turban and a heavy cloak. His eyes look fierce, and he has a thick moustache that drapes over his lips and onto his graying beard. Persian men like him used to pluck a mustache hair and offer it to their debtor as a sign of their honor. These were bold men who fought for what they believed. It was like a dagger in their heart if their personal honor was ever compromised.

Within its frame, Abolghassem's image looks back across time and geography, across two generations . . . across a space that looms larger than anything I can hold in my mind. As Khan Daee once asked, what *would* Abolghassem think of his Americanized progeny living so far from his homeland? He'd probably shudder with disgust. I do not think he would be proud of any of us, as we are of him: the man who fought for the sovereignty of his beloved Iran.

Abolghassem was committed to his citizenship, a *vatan parast,* homeland worshipper. I can't say that about myself. Immigrant children don't have that sort of bond to any land. Once you transplant your roots, they never again get a firm hold.

49

At least mine did not. And so I look at my great-grandfather's photograph and puzzle over what it might be that I have inherited from him, if anything at all. Moman tells me that she has no doubt that his blood flows through at least one of my veins. Abolghassem's thunderous temper earned him his sobriquet. To everyone, including his progeny, he is known as the vilified religious persona of the Shi'ite faith: *Shimr.*

* * *

In 632 AD, the prophet Muhammed died. Since he had not specified a successor, his demise created a power vacuum. The fledgling Islamic community needed a Khalifa (Caliph), someone to become prophet Muhammed's "viceroy," his "substitute," a representative of Allah on earth. Vicious battles to determine who would assume stewardship of the Islamic community ensued. Some argued that the successor to the messenger to God (meaning the Prophet Muhammed) should be elected. They said the "commander of the faithful" should be the one who is most capable. This group selected Muhammed's father-in-law, Abu Bakr, to be the first Caliphate. Meanwhile, others believed that the prophet's son-in-law, Ali, should assume the leadership of their faith. Since the prophet did not have a son, this group deemed Ali the closest family member and thus the obvious heir to leadership of their religion.The power structure of the franchise, disputed along this ideological rift, eventually charted Islam's two main branches: the Sunnis, who favored Abu Bakr, and the Shi'ites, who favored Ali. Disagreement between these two groups has marked the pages of history with many scenes of bloodshed. Perhaps none is memorialized more by Shi'ites than the battle of Karbalā.

The battle of Karbalā took place in 680 AD. The Prophet Muhammed's grandson, the legendary Islamic figure Husayn ibn 'Alī, was struggling to create a regime that would reinstate a "true" Islamic polity. Husayn opposed what he considered the undevine rule of the Umayyad, the second of four caliphates.

Under Umayyad, the Muslim empire had expanded rapidly: to the west it encompassed North Africa and Spain; to the east it reached as far as India. Umayyad was a formidable ruler, and Husayn versus Umayyad mirrored David and Goliath. Nevertheless, Husayn pressed forward to claim leadership of the Muslims and to take them back to their hereditary roots, which he believed belonged to his paternal grandfather. Thus the battle of Karbalā resulted:

> *It is said that on October 10, 680 (Muharram 10, 61 AH), Husayn and a small group of his followers and family members, numbering seventy-two or more, engaged in a battle with Umayyad's army of perhaps thirty thousand men. Husayn and all of his men were killed and beheaded. Their bodies were left for three days without burial, and survivors from Husayn's family were taken as prisoners to al-Sham (Syria and Lebanon today). In this gruesome scene of slaughter, Husayn is said to have been beheaded by the commander of Umayyad's army, Shimr Ibn Thil-Jawshan.Iranians, who are predominately Shi'ite, know him simply as Shimr, a name that evokes fear, hatred, ruthlessness.*

And it is this name—Shimr—that Abolghassem Karbassi came to be known by, though arguably it was tinged with an element of reverence and adoration.

Kerman
1920
"Boroh gomsho"
"Inglisi!"
"Pedar Saag"

Insults rain down on the white man sitting backwards on a mule. A laborer holds the mule's reins while two men stand at either side. Moments earlier, Dr. Dodson, a 35-year-old British missionary and medical doctor, had been working at the site of the new hospital, reviewing plans. Two men grabbed him and a crowd gathered. Now he sits on a mule, facing a big man waving a thick, elegantly carved wooden staff. The big man looms over the other with his thick beard and moustache; his bushy brows canopy his fierce eyes. His long black cloak touches the ground, a golden-colored embroidered silk turban sits on his head.

The big man is shouting at the doctor. But when he turns to face the crowd, everyone shrinks back. His wrath spills over all of them.

"Lo . . . lot . . ." Dr. Dodson stutters, trying to remember any Farsi words he has learned. "*Lotfaan*, please, what have I done?" Three weeks in Iran, one week in Kerman, and suddenly all is lost—his dream of converting heathens to Christ by helping the sick . . . maybe even his life.

"Pedar Saag, son of a dog!" Abolghassem thunders at the white man with wispy blonde hair. Abolghassem turns to the crowd. "This man is the son of the dogs who sneak into our homes and steal—yes, do you hear me? They steal our land— they steal our oil. Did they come to fight us like men?"

"No," the crowd answers emphatically.

"No, they are not men. They are jackals, vermin—sneaking in the night. Dogs in blue uniforms carrying rifles. They steal our sons!"

Abolghassem slams his staff to the ground several times and shouts, "This is *our* country!"

The crowd bursts into cheers.

"And who let these dogs in?"

There is no answer from the crowd. Eyes dart around—you never know who could be listening.

"You all know—you know as well I do." Abolghassem points his staff at the crowd. He appears ready to charge, "And not one of you has the guts to say it . . ."

"Infidels," someone shouts.

"Infidels! The donkey's ass is an infidel. Did the British dogs ride in on the ass of the ass?"

Feet shift uneasily.

Abolghassem turns to the crowd. As if standing on a pulpit, he begins to deliver a scathing harangue to the man on top of the mule—or at least what the man represents to his beloved Iran. Striding up and down with the giant steps of a panther and gesticulating with a pointed finger, he shouts: "Yes, you are cowards not to say it. All of you! Every man here knows the truth—the degenerate who sleeps with foreigners, who lets the British dogs piss on him and who stabs us in the back—yes, the Shah! Do you hear me? Ahmad Shah Qajar. That despicable child who we call our monarch! He was a child when he was handed the throne. He still is a child, twenty-two years old and running a country? No, he's always frolicking in Europe! I have said it, and I say come and arrest me—now! You know me, I went to prison for all of you and I will go again—for Iran! Who here will stand with me for Iran?"

In the early years of the twentieth century, Abolghassem watched as foreign powers encircled Iran. He saw how weak and corrupt the Shah had been. He chose to fight—not against the British, but against the government that had sold out his country and abandoned the legacy of the Persian warriors. Abolghassem knew history, but he kept a keen eye on the future. He fought for constitutional rule in Iran. He fought for democracy and the rights of his people. He opposed the Shah and the religious clerics.

At that time, Iran was ablaze with democratic debates. Although only in his early thirties, Abolghassem was already powerful, wealthy, and outspoken. He joined a political group called the National Democrats, which was holding clandestine meetings all over the country to determine how to rid Iran of the corrupt Qajar dynasty. Abolghassem was one of nine men in the secret National Democrat Committee in Kerman. To hide their identities, they had adopted code names. His fellow committee members came to call Abolghassem "Shimr." They thought it fit his thunderous character.

The National Democrats were nationalists and wanted to give the people a voice and power. They wanted their country to have democratic processes, a constitution, and a parliament. They opposed not only the Qajar dynasty but also the Islamic factions that sought to replace the monarchy with *ulama,* rule by the Islamic clerics.

The local clerics struck back by denouncing Abolghassem as a Baha'i, the religious sect that grew out of Islam in Iran in the nineteenth century. Members of the Baha'i faith were often executed for heresy. But such rumors about Abolghassem went unheeded. Everyone knew Abolghassem: he was outspoken, he was passionate, he was a shrewd businessman, and he was *not* religious. In fact, Abolghassem, like his forefathers, held Islam in contempt. Four generations back, his great-great grandfather, Ahmad Zardoshti, had been forced to covert from Zoroastrianism to Islam. Through the generations, resentment was passed down from father to son. A sort of apathy. Or one could say, a tacit resignation of one's faith. Maybe it was for this reason that Abolghassem, fiery and passionate, was interested not in religion but in politics. He was a member of the National Democrats for twenty years, during which time he and eight other influential Kermani businessmen operated under secret code names. His was "Shimr." With the country sharply divided between monarchists and clerics seeking ulama, on the path to democracy was a dangerous place to be.

People seeking power fear a man like Abolghassem. He was well read and informed about the world and its history. He was independently wealthy due to his legendary carpet-making and to his skill investing in and managing land. Even more dangerous for those in power, Abolghassem was an independent thinker who did not seek approval from others. He spoke his mind regardless of the cost. In a society that prized obedience, Abolghassem chose not to follow but to lead. Like a warrior who knows the costs of battle, he accepted the risks of his outspoken views. In 1905, the local clerics turned him in. He was arrested and served five years in Shiraz as a political prisoner.

Abolghassem was sitting in a Shiraz compound for political prisoners when the news of Iran's constitutional victory reached him in 1906. His country had won its first battle for a constitutional decree and the creation of a *majlis,* an elected parliament. While serving out his sentence, Abolghassem felt gratified that the work of the National Democrats had paid off, that the will of his people had succeeded over both the monarchy and the clerics.

"Boroh gomsho, inglisi—go, get lost. Go back to your bastard land," Abolghassem roars again. His face reddened with anger, Abolghassem then turns from the stupefied doctor to the laborer holding the mule harness and barks his orders in a stentorian voice: "Take the white dog foreign bastard to Bandar Abbas. At the port, he can find his way back to his own country. Take him away." He puts a coin in the sunburned man's open palm.

The laborer smiles and says obediently, *"Chashm Agha."* He clicks his tongue and nudges his mule onto the road toward Bandar Abbas.

Abolghassem shouts out his final instruction, "Keep him on the mule all the way to the gulf. Let him piss in his pants, not on our land." Then, turning to the crowd, "That white skin's gone— never to be seen again. He is the first. We will drive out all of the white dogs."

Abolghassem strides through the remaining crowd, which reverently and fearfully opens a path for him.

Dr. Dodson struggles to stay on the mule as he watches the big man walk away and the town of Kerman return to normal. He is stunned. One moment, he was engrossed in planning documents. Then, in a flash, he was swept up in a near riot. Now he clings to a mule picking its way out of town. He doesn't know if the man in the gold silk turban has saved his life or banished him to death in the desert. Long after Kerman has disappeared from view, he turns around on the mule and faces the dirt road ahead. At the next town, he pays off the laborer, buying his freedom. Another man might have left Iran to sail back to the safety of England and a lucrative medical practice. He might have secured a country estate where, resting his feet on a prized Persian carpet, he could have gestured to the carpet and entertained his guests with the story of his near death in Kerman, the home of the greatest masters of the Persian carpets.

Persian carpets often embody stories about the great feats of Persian heroes: Jamshid Shah standing in front of a mighty Persian army, the seven labors of Rostam, magnificent kings leading armies into battle, horsemen engaged in the ancient Persian sport of *shogun bazi,* polo. These are the stories that run through the soul of Abolghassem. The Persian warrior is heroic—worthy of the legends woven into his nation's carpets. No power could vanquish the Persian warrior—not the Mongols of Genghis Khan nor the Ottomans.

And, unknown to Dr. Dodson, Abolghassem—the man in the gold turban—is the artist and master of Persian carpets. His designs and the vivid colors of his dyes—preserved in the intricate knots that will last for centuries—pay homage to the Persian character: fearless, enduring, stubborn, passionate, and proud.

Abolghassem makes rugs for palaces and grand halls near and far: for viziers and tsars, for kings and chancellors. In 1903, Abolghassem made a carpet commissioned by the Congress of the United States of America that set his work aside from all the rest. It took his team of skillful weavers four years to complete the largest carpet ever created: it measured 75 feet in length and 45 feet in width.

Abolghassem's rugs are national treasures. His skill is legendary. Russians, Greeks, and Egyptians send their craftsmen to Kerman to learn from the master.

His work has brought him both fame and wealth. He has bought farmland, on which he grows fruit and pistachios. As befits a wealthy man, he has two wives and six children, three by each wife. His first wife, Bibi Syedeh, has given him two sons, Mahmoud and Kazem, and one daughter, Esmat. As his first wife, she lives in his large estate. His second wife, Bibi Fatemeh, lives in a small house on the far side of Kerman in a less-than-dignified neighborhood. She had been a widow for many years and already had a daughter when Abolghassem took her as his second wife. Bibi Fatemeh bore two sons by Abolghassem, Ahmad and Mehdy.

As Abolghassem strides through the crowd back to his compound, the two sons by his second wife are waiting, wearing the blue uniforms of the South Persian Rifles.

* * *

The British are a new type of enemy. They have invaded without amassing their armies on the field of battle. This British invasion began July 25, 1872, when Nasr al-Din, Shah of the Qajar Dynasty, signed a seventy-year concession allowing Britain to exploit Iran's mineral resources. Twenty-nine years later, in 1901, Britain's emissaries force the corrupt Nasr al-Din Shah to sell his country out once again and by extending Britain's right to exploitation for another sixty years. And a mere six years later, as Britain moves its pawns throughout the world to secure its leverage in Europe, the British and Russians sign the Anglo-Russian agreement. Without Iran's consent or knowledge, Britain claim the oil of southern Iran and Russia secures the strategic trading points of northern Iran.

When the Great War arrives in 1914, the British tighten their hold on southern Iran. A grip that is made tighter in 1917 when the Communist Revolution collapses the Russian monarchy. The British rival is forced to abandon its interest in northern Iran. The Bolsheviks withdraw Russian troops from Iran to defend the Revolution. Consequently, Britain is left alone to completely dominate Iran. By the winter of the last year of the war, 1918-19, Britain's power in Iran is at its zenith. The British Empire stretches from the Indian Ocean to the Himalayas to the Caucasus; Iran serves a critical link for Britain.

The British are savvy colonizers. In India they effectively use Indian nationals to police the country on Britain's behalf. Though Iran is never officially a British colony, a similar tactic is used there. Under the guise of national safety, the British create the South Persian Rifles, enlisting young Iranian men by force. They are trained, armed, fed, and clad in blue uniforms. Their orders are to patrol their own towns under the command of British officers.

Over the course of his life, Abolghassem sees the British sneaking into his country inch by inch, first stealing Iranian oil, then they gain control of the Persian treasury, then they take Iran's very land itself, and now they are stealing the sons of Kerman—stealing his own sons.

* * *

Abolghassem had heard a rumor one morning that two of his sons had joined the Persian Rifles. When he summoned Ahmad and Mehdy to his home, they appeared wearing the blue British uniform, their heads bowed. The rumor was true. His sons had put a knife in his back in the form of two blue tunics. Abolghassem could not speak. He left the house with his cape blowing behind him, his staff punching the air. Around the bend from his estate a hospital was being built, this is where came across Dr. Dodson mulling over some sheets of paper. It was this sight that unleashed his anger. Dodson was the first Brit to cross his path since he received the news about his sons. Abolghassem had ordered two men to grab the missionary and put him on a mule.

Now he had driven out one English dog, but he still had two sons at home.

Ahmad and Mehdy do not seem to have moved since Abolghassem left. They are kneeling on the rug at the foot of the courtyard, still wearing the blue tunics.

From the gate of his house, Abolghassem bellows to his sons, "How dare you humiliate me?"

Ahmad turns to face his father and says pointedly, "Pedar, father, we have no choice. You know very well they are forcing us to join the cavalry."

Abolghassem fires back, "Mahmoud hasn't joined!" Mahmoud has fled to the mountains to fight the British.

"Mahmoud is only hiding in the Saheb al-zaman Mountains! He'll have to come back sooner or later," Ahmad says.

"He is a fighter! You are cowards! British cowards. Persian men are brave. We drove out the Mongols. We will drive out the British—but not with pathetic dogs like you."

Ahmad and Mehdy keep their heads down. Mahmoud, their half-brother, has become a hero in Kerman. People leave food for Mahmoud and his band by the roadside near the mountains. They are freedom fighters. But Ahmad and Mehdy? People in Kerman sneer at them when they pass in their uniforms. They hear the word "traitors" hissed behind their backs.

"I went to prison for fighting for our country. And what do my own sons do? You destroy my work. I spit on your faces, you ungrateful beasts."

Then suddenly there is silence. Abolghassem strokes his right palm across the rug on which they are sitting, one of the earliest carpets his rug-makers made, nearly three decades earlier. As he moves his hand across the rug's surface, the three sit quietly, looking at its rich colors created by natural dyes, as vibrant as though woven only days ago. With knots so small and tight, the carpet will last long after any of them has breath to breathe.

Bringing his hand to a stop on the intricate floral design that distinguishes it as one of his rugs, Abolghassem speaks in a solemn voice.

"From this day on, you two are no longer my sons."

The gravity of his words hangs in the air and then slowly settles on all three.

"From now on, you are banished from my home, from my inheritance, from my life. Mahmoud is my only heir! *Hala gomshin,* now get lost!"

After a few minutes of silence, Ahmad and Mehdy rise reluctantly and bow. They put on the boots they left by the side of the rug and head toward the courtyard gates. Before they reach the gate, Ahmad looks at his father's turned back and hesitates briefly. He has never been able to stand up to his father and so desperately wants to do so now. He seems ready to move back to his father when Mehdy grabs his hand and pushes him out the door. They leave, never to be welcomed in their father's house again.

* * *

It's 1925. Iran has a new Shah: Reza Khan. First ruler of the Pahlavi dynasty. Once commander of the Persian Cossack brigade, Reza Khan seizes power in 1923, and two years later crowns himself
the new Shah. He has seen firsthand the weakness of Iran at the hands of the military powers of Great Britain and Russia. Their domination and manipulation has been intolerable to him. To strengthen Iran is more than a military task to Reza Khan. He intends to force Iran into the modern world, perhaps following in the footsteps of the new Turkish leader, Mustafia Kemal "Ataturk."

Reza Khan has set out to build a new Iran. He builds a trans-Iranian railroad, concretes highways, builds schools and hospitals. He asks the international community not to call the country Persia but Iran, "land of Aryans." He issues a series of decrees that include instituting a code of justice and providing education for women. His decrees reach into every corner of Iranian life, from banning the veil to forcing every head of a household to adopt a family name that is passed down from father to son on an official birth certificate. Iran's patronymic system, Reza Khan declares, is an impediment to progress.

When word reaches Kerman in 1927 that heads of households are to adopt a surname, Abolghassem gathers his family. In attendance are some seventy male relations. On that day, Abolghassem announces his decision. Henceforth, his descendants carry the name Karbassi, born from and belonging to karbass, which is a burlap cloth produced in Kerman. The fabric is cool to the skin, refreshing in the hot desert air. A strong fabric that breathes. Karbass resists condensation, making it strong enough to endure and to protect what is wrapped inside. Endurance and protection, the lessons of desert survival. Abolghassem has decided that this textile, like his carpets, shall represent him in posterity. All male members, save his two sons, Ahmad and Mehdy, are asked to adopt Karbassi as the family name.

Kerman
1936

On a dark, windy January afternoon, Abolghassem falls in the middle of his courtyard.

His son, Mahmoud, hears the first cry: "Aghay-e Karbassi! Hurry!"

Mahmoud doesn't wait for an explanation. He flies across the courtyard and down the street. Without thinking, Reza runs after him.

In the cries of alarm, Reza hears a name: his grandfather's.

He is running, running blindly toward his grandfather's home. The doors are wide open. There are shouts and wails. Mahmoud is barking orders. The neighbors are crowded into the courtyard. The winds are ripping through the alleyways. In the chaos, Reza sees only one thing: Abolghassem's fallen body on the cold stones of the courtyard.

He hears a carriage coming, hoofbeats pounding.

Mahmoud directs four men to lift the body into the carriage. Mahmoud clings to the side. A whip cracks and the carriage is gone.

Sheykh-Javad, one of Abolghassem's most trusted weavers, was speaking to him right before he fell. The two had just finished discussing dye shades for the carpet commissioned by Reza Khan. Sheykh-Javad is now standing and talking to anyone who will listen. He had just spoken to Abolghassem—"about dyes—he wanted the shade different—the red—no, the blue dye wasn't right—he always knew—he was right there—I turned away—a moment and I heard a thump and he was there—on the ground—like the wind just knocked him over . . ."

Sheykh-Javad lives with his wife and children in Abolghassem's compound in a room they call *rang-rezi,* where they prepare and store vats of dyes for rugs. Young Reza listens to the old man like he is listening to a bird—he hears sounds but no meaning. He feels ripped open—like the winds were sweeping through him, stealing everything inside him. The central column of a great mosque has crumbled.

Out of the fog of sound, Reza catches one word: "alive." He was alive when they put him in the carriage! Reza runs out of the courtyard, along the dusty alleyways to the hospital, Morselin Hospital. He finds his father, Mahmoud. "He's alive. But he's not fully conscious," his father tells him.

Reza doesn't know what that means, but he nods gravely.

A British doctor enters the room, fair skinned with blonde hair. He reaches out his hand and, in impeccable Farsi, introduces himself to Mahmoud.

"I am Dr. Dodson, and you are the son? Very well, Aghay-e Karbassi, shall we see the patient?"

The three enter the room. Abolghassem lies unconscious in the hospital bed. Dr. Dodson greets Abolghassem, even though the patient cannot respond.

Dr. Dodson then turns to Mahmoud, "I know this man, he sent me on the longest donkey ride I ever had."

Mahmoud knows the story from sixteen years earlier, but he has no emotion to spare. He searches the British man's eyes for any desire for revenge.

Dr. Dodson smiles gently, placing his hand on Mahmoud's shoulder. "I will do everything I can to save your father."

Abolghassem lies on a bed at Morselin Hospital, under Dr. Dodson's care, in the hospital built by Dr. Dodson and the British. Each day, Reza walks with his father to the hospital to see Abolghassem. They sit in the hospital room for long hours. Often, the only sound is the slow, labored breathing of a body in a bed. Abolghassem no longer seems like the great man, the grandfather Reza knew.

Reza studies the face of his grandfather with its stonelike, deeply chiseled features. Here is a man of power, who even when simply walking sweeps ahead of others, whose voice is commanding. Even the clerics fear him. He is a man who talks about the world with knowledge, who sends his creations to faraway places like Russia, Egypt, France, and America. And he knows Persia with the intimate knowledge of a patriot. Reza has listened to the stories of Rostam recited by Abolghassem through the poetry of Ferdowsi. It seems to Reza that his grandfather had fought beside Rostam and had tea with Ferdowsi.

But now his grandfather is silent—his churning energy stilled.

One day, Dr. Dodson meets Mahmoud and Reza outside the room. Once again his hand clasps Mahmoud's shoulder.

Abolghassem died at sunrise on a March morning in 1936.

It is the first time in his life that Reza feels loss.

Chapter 5
Vatan Parast

Would Abolghassem have considered my father a worthless coward and disowned him, as he did with his own sons? It's something of an irony that what Abolghassem despised kept reappearing among his own brood. This reminds me of a proverb my mother recites:

> *Shotor har chi az ader badesh miad, gusheh labesh sabz misheh.*
> As much as a camel hates thorny plants, it seeds itself on the corner of its lips.

And yet I wonder, would Abolghassem have found compassion for my father if he knew what his circumstances were in 1979, when the Islamic Revolution in Iran put the country in the hands of religious clerics? Wouldn't Abolghassem consider mullahs another enemy, just like the foreigners he once said stole Iran's riches from his people? Hasn't the current so-called religious government stolen from Iranians too, only this time under the cloak of religion? Aren't they just another enemy in disguise? Was Baba a coward for staying in the United States, or too proud to live under what he called "backward-thinking mullahs?" Would Abolghassem consider my father a traitor or a nationalist?

I argue that Baba was—in his own way—*vatan parast*.

But this I discovered only recently. I didn't realize the depths of my father's predicament—whether to go back to Iran or to stay here in this country—until I started writing this book. It's only now, in hindsight, that I realize what Baba—as a father—must have gone through. Back then I was a teenager dealing with my own issues—being the only brown-skinned girl in an ocean of fair-skinned, blue-eyed girls in Narragansett, Rhode Island. The lone foreigner trying to blend in at Narragansett High School. Our worries were different, my father and I. Only now do I realize the weight he was carrying.

**Narragansett
2005**

Akhtar opens the faucet to a little more than a trickle. She puts a drop of dishwashing liquid onto an overused sponge and wipes the barely soiled breakfast plates. The only kitchen window is cracked open and the chirping of Narragansett's summer birds floods in. The neighbor's lawn is lush green and meticulously mowed. The shrubbery is neatly trimmed and the flowers, in mulched beds, are vibrant and cheery.

Akhtar and Reza's lawn looks shabby, with its overgrown weeds and bald spots. Reza used to mow the lawn regularly. Reza wanted his lawn to look like the neighbor's. Donning a baseball cap and sweat clothes, he felt fully American as he pushed his power mower back and forth across the yard. After conquering the lawn, he would come in for a cold beer, then switch on the shortwave radio to hear the news from Iran. The superficial feeling of being red, white and blue faded quickly.

It has been a couple of years since Reza last mowed the lawn. His Parkinson's disease keeps him from it, or maybe he no longer wants to feel American, not even for a moment. Their shaggy, patchy yard makes Akhtar feel separated from the neighbors, as if she were back in Tehran looking at the picture of Khan Daee's California lawn—a mystical green lawn in a distant, unreachable land. She can see the line where the beautiful lawns next door abut their own rough grass and weeds. The line might as well have been the ocean that lies between Iran and America, for despite years of living side-by-side, she knows nothing about her neighbors. They know nothing about her.

Reza always said, "It's good that people here mind their own business. They do their own thing. Not like us Iranians, always meddlesome."

Akhtar sees it differently. The gulf between the two houses makes her feel empty. She craves an environment where her neighbors and extended family are a part of her daily life. She used to tolerate being lonesome. After all, their stay in America was only temporary. But as the years wore on and the prospect of returning home receded from her hopes, she learned to play a different mind game. She imagined the day when her children would marry and have kids of their own. Then, she hoped, her family would surround her and the sound of chatter and laughter would at last break her loneliness.

She rinses the last spoon and turns off the tap. Reza is still struggling to make his way to the living room. He seems to freeze every few steps. The clock on the countertop microwave reads seven thirty, prompting her to hasten to get to the pile of boxes waiting to be sorted in the garage. But first she walks over and puts her right leg in front of Reza's frozen feet. She puts her leg right in his line of vision to trick his nervous system into connecting with the mind. Sudden loud noise works too. Sometimes she shouts at him.

His feet snap back into step. He makes his way to a high-backed armchair and slowly sinks into the seat, releasing a sigh of exhaustion.

"Karbassi, do you want me to bring you the box of papers?"

"*Areh,* put it here," he says, pointing to the foot of his chair. His dark olive skin is now softened to an ashy white of old age. He still commands Akhtar, but more and more Akhtar must tell him what to do. With hunched shoulders, quivering hands, and stiffened joints, he takes his bifocals from a wooden side table, slips them on, and slowly adjusts himself in his chair. He patiently waits for Akhtar to return with the files he needs to go through. A few minutes pass before Akhtar places a box next to Reza's chair and then heads back to the garage. Reza takes a folder, labeled in the neat, precise handwriting he had before Parkinson's robbed him of control of his hand. The folder reads, "Immigration & Naturalization."

Reza saved every page of the paperwork for his application for U.S. citizenship, as if having more pages made him more American. He worried that he might someday be told he wasn't American enough—that he had forgotten some slip of paper that held the proof.

* * *

In 1979, it seemed that every Iranian in the U.S. was trying to become a citizen. Overnight, the elite from the Shah era were fleeing from Iran to America, close behind them the followers of the non-Islamic religions who had been living in Iran. Ayatollah Khomeini's new Islamic regime brought to Iran a wave of violence and a panicked exodus.

At that time, the United States was caught up in the hostage crisis. The network news anchors were counting the days that university students held 52 American citizens hostage. Every night, the television showed the streets of Tehran full of angry students shouting, "Death to America." Hatred seemed to spill out of the television, coloring Americans' view of every Iranian. Day by day, the count of the hostage crisis in Iran grew, not ending until day 444.

It wasn't safe to be an American in Iran. But was it any safer to be an Iranian in America? Reza was a hostage to the crisis too. He couldn't go home, but without a valid visa, he couldn't stay in the U.S.

He regularly climbed the stairs of the INS office in Providence. An old woman, reeking of stale cigarette smoke, dismissed him with a wave. He thanked her, then took a chair and waited. Reza watched the clock above the American flag hanging on the wall. He waited as the clock moved forward, first minutes, then hours. He waited in the office till closing, then he went home and came back the next day, waiting and waiting as the weeks became months. Every petition was denied. Months became years. Reza waited over 1,400 days, suspended in limbo between legal residency and expulsion back to Iran.

He exhausted every avenue. He was denied his petition to become a permanent resident, his green card, even a work visa. After nearly four years of waiting in uncertainty, he had one last option: to seek political asylum.

His Boston-based lawyer, Mr. O'Neill, told him that, except for communist dissidents, political asylum was almost never granted. He stressed that Reza's only chance was to prove beyond a doubt that his life would be in danger if he returned to Iran. He had to demonstrate not only why his life was threatened, but how. But, as Mr. O'Neill said, "It was worth a shot." At the very least, filing for political asylum would buy them extra time in the U.S. Reza was sure that his petition would be denied and force his family to return to a turbulent and uncertain life in Iran.

Reza's sole evidence was the photograph of him kissing the hand of the Shah.

On a sunny day in June 1983, Reza's petition finally came before an immigration judge. The day was warm, but Reza's hand felt cold and clammy. Akhtar sat to his left, his daughter and son sat behind him. Keyhan, his eldest son, was stuck in Iran. Mr. O'Neill sat on his right.

The government's lawyer sat beyond Mr. O'Neill, at a separate table.

In front of both tables, sitting up high behind a polished mahogany desk, was the judge. The small courtroom had a hushed air of grandeur and authority. The walls were paneled in a rich brown wood. Portraits of venerable white men, their brows chiseled in serious thought, hung all around the room. Reza felt as though he were sitting in the cradle of the modern, civilized world—something he had always idealized and related to in America. Yet, he could not fend off a sense of dread. This was his last try.

Mr. O'Neill presented Reza's case, finally offering the photograph as "pivotal" proof. He slid it across the smooth tabletop to the judge. The judge furrowed his brows as he carefully inspected it: a simple black-and-white picture of Reza in his white shirt and black tie, bowing to kiss the Pahlavi monarch's hand. The Shah is looking off into the distance, oblivious to Reza.

The young state department lawyer looked appalled. "This case is simply inadequate," the lawyer said. "How could this man claim that his life could ever be threatened? One photograph with the Shah proves nothing. Look, the Shah doesn't even know him."

Reza shuddered. He agreed with the lawyer. He wasn't an associate of the Shah—he merely supported him, as did most Iranians before the Revolution. He was caught: he was in danger in Iran because he worked for the Shah, but he couldn't stay in America because he wasn't close enough to the deposed monarch. The mere thought of backwards-thinking mullahs running the country made him sick to his stomach.

The judge agreed with the state department lawyer. "I agree that this case does not fall under the tenets of an asylum." Reza had waited four years for this. He sat tense and upright as the judge continued: "Even though this application's claims are weak, I cannot see, in good judgment, why we don't extend to this seemingly decent family the right to reside in this country."

The judge peered through the top of his glasses at Reza and his family. "Isn't that all they are seeking?" the judge asked. Then the judge smiled for the first time. "I'll be going on vacation tomorrow, my first after three years, and this is my last case. Let's end the day on a positive note, shall we?"

He rapped his gavel and announced, "I hereby approve Reza Karbassi's application."

Reza was speechless. Had he heard right? Mr. O'Neill was standing in front of him, pumping his hand and congratulating him. Slowly, Reza realized that what he thought was impossible had come true.

* * *

Holding the file in his hands, Reza can still feels the intense relief that he felt on that day twenty-five years ago. With the judge's word he was freed from limbo. He felt proud that he was now a member of the society that he idealized. He could work legally in the U.S. He did not have to return to Iran, which was now embroiled in a bloody war with Iraq.

However, he also realized that the judge's signature on the application slammed shut the doors to Iran. His oldest son was trapped there. They could not return safely to see him. "Not while this group of religious idiots running the country is there," he'd say to Akhtar.

Shifting on his chair, he holds the file over the trash bucket that Akhtar has set beside his chair for this task. His hands tremble. For some reason, the file feels heavier than it should, as though it carries the burden the asylum case placed on them. A prisoner's ball and chain. The file freed him to stay here, but it prevented his return to Iran. The new Islamic government could accuse him of nothing. He merely worked under the Shah. But, his application for political asylum was proof that he was hiding his ties to the former regime. Any link to the Shah was dangerous in those days.

Like his friend Dr. Reyazi. Reyazi was an educator, the president of Tehran's Technical College. He had no role in politics and little connection with the Shah. After the Revolution, he stayed in Switzerland to weather the political chaos in Iran. But he longed for home and believed he had nothing to fear— after all, he ran a school. "The new government will need schools, and they need me," he thought. So Dr. Reyazi returned to Tehran to a joyous reunion with his family. Three days later, he was arrested and executed. No formal charges were ever filed against him. His only "crime" was that he had served the former regime.

The fate of Dr. Reyazi and many other friends and acquaintances were proof enough for Reza that it was not safe to go back to Iran, especially with a political asylum case condemning him as a traitor to the Revolution.

The case contained in the fat folder he now holds in his hands had kept him alive, but also kept him in America for far longer than he envisioned.

Reza hesitates, and then lets it fall with a thump into the metal trash can. He is surprised at how easy it is to let it go. Peering down into the can, he sees papers scattered, like the cadaver of a beast finally put to rest.

The thump of the file as Reza drops it in the bin echoes down the hallway. It catches Akhtar's attention. It's the immigration file, she's sure. How odd, she thinks, that it could be flicked away so easily, when twenty-five years ago, every detail, every filing, every letter, held their lives in the balance.

She sighs, blessing and cursing that folder at the same time.

Chapter 6
Curse

Children of immigrants, like me, often get confused about their identity. When you grow up in America with parents of another nationality . . . of another *land* . . . there's a duality that lives within you. There are two sides to you, and sometimes you're not sure who is who. You have a warped sense of identity. There is what is seen/done/felt at home, and what is seen/done/felt in the "outside" world. Your identity is lodged somewhere in between. Especially with a father like mine, who on the one hand adored America and Americans, but on the other hand was always glued to his shortwave radio hoping for the slightest news that would enable him to go back to Iran.

"We're neither here nor there," Moman says. *Our happiness is neither here nor there,* is probably more accurate. We seem to suffer from a terminal sense of limbo. A curse of sorts.

So it's inevitable that I ask what put us in this state. What made Baba reach for America and the American dream? What in his past led him here?

Writing the tale of my parents' migration required me to go back to the precise moments that I think defined my parents' destiny. For my mother, I'd argue it was the day that Sadegh told her whom she would live with for the rest of her life. For my father, it was a moment even more somber.

Kerman
1940

Kerman's bazaar is strangely quiet. Gone is the usual crowd of shoppers bustling along the marketplace's snaking passageways. The mules stand with empty backs. Gone is the sound of their hooves clicking on cobblestones. Gone is the beehive of marketing frenzy. Vendors no longer holler, competing to be heard above the others' voices as they boast about their goods, scooping sundries from gunny sacks—burlap—perched on the stony bazaar grounds. The sellers have little to offer, and the buyers have little to spend. Far beyond the borders of Iran, the world's war machines consume all commodities. Even though Iran has declared neutrality, it feels the impact of the world's crisis: WWII. Scarcity and rationing have hit the nation. Sugar, flour, and oil are hard to come by these days. Even kerosene, the lifeline of this oil-rich nation, is in tight supply. Scarcity breeds despair in Kerman. Eyes take on the look of hunger. And when the eyes are hungry, the Kermoonis believe, "Beware the man of fortune." Wistful looks become edged with bitterness, and soon the hungry eye becomes the "evil eye," unleashing its revenge.

* * *

Behind the high brick walls surrounding his grand property, Mahmoud has built the first brick house in Kerman. His neighbors' houses are made of mud. The large courtyard has two wading pools. The one by the main house is ornately tiled. Across the courtyard are the servants' quarters, with their own wading pool. The carpet weavers work on the west side of the property, while on the east side are the orchards of walnut, pomegranate, and apricot. The wooden front gate opens onto a narrow dirt alleyway that winds its way to Kerman's ancient bazaar, and to the tenth-century Masjid Malik, the Mosque of the King.

Mahmoud abandoned the rebel life in the mountains long ago and is now a recognized rug-maker, like his father, Abolghassem. Mahmoud's business and leadership skills have enabled him to build a sizable fortune. His lavish house is in the affluent community of Masjid Malik, named after the mosque.

Within Mahmoud's compound is a separate, serene world, which is undisturbed by the war and scarce resources.

This afternoon, like every other afternoon, a servant unrolls a paisley print carpet and spreads out large, hand-embroidered cylinder pillows. Mahmoud, barefoot and wearing a white linen gown, stretches comfortably against the pillows, one hand on the mouthpiece of a water pipe and the other brushing away flies.

Nearby, 13-year-old Reza kneels by the edge of the rug doing his homework. His two younger sisters skip rope on the courtyard stones. Four-year-old Javad, the youngest, clings to his mother, Soghra.

Soghra sits cross-legged, with the layers of her skirt folded on her lap. Modestly dressed, she wears a scarf and a single gold chain with a gold emblem bearing the name of Allah. She is devout, even though her husband derides Islam. She believes that her faith protects her family. She observes daily prayer and religious holidays. Each year, during the mourning period with which Shi'ite Muslims commemorate the seventh-century martyrdom of Imam Husayn, Soghra holds a grand *nazr* ceremony to pray for the health of her children, her sons in particular.

She orders twelve candles made to match her son Reza's height. On the tenth night of the mourning period, dressed all in black, Reza walks in a procession through the neighborhood, with servants carrying the candles by his side. The pageant ends at the old tree near the mosque of Masjid Malik. There, beneath the tree, Soghra and her servants ladle food to the poor, a blessed meal made from a slaughtered lamb. She lives in the rhythm of Islam, asking God to protect her sons.

Soghra is an unusual woman—she can read. She was educated by tutors hired by her father, a widower and owner of a prosperous cotton-cleaning business. She was her father's only child and he lavished his love on her. He was proud of her literacy, of the fact that she would write letters and complete forms for their illiterate neighbors. Nevertheless, he married his daughter to Mahmoud when she was fifteen and Mahmoud was thirty.

As Soghra obeys God, so she obeys her husband. She serves both every day. This afternoon, as every afternoon, she carefully lines the inside of the silver brazier with coal pellets. She fills the brazier, her sooty hands methodically arranging the coal. A servant brings her a small batch of embers from the kitchen. Placing them at the center of the brazier, she waves a straw fan until the coal chunks begin to glow a fiery red. The embers are now ready for the opium.

She places the brazier with its burning embers next to Mahmoud. With effort, she lifts herself off the rug and heads toward the cooking area to supervise the dinner. Small and frail, Javad, trails behind her. Soghra's father died while she was pregnant with Javad. Her father's death devastated her. She wept endlessly, and her pregnancy was tainted with her sorrow. Sometimes it seems to her that her son has the spirit of her father: Javad is always right by her side. Like her father, Javad seems to need her constant presence, as if it were only the two of them in the world. Javad even seems to share her grief in losing her father, his physical weakness embodying the loss his mother has failed to accept.

In the kitchen, the large cooking pots simmer on open fires. Soghra samples from each and then sends a trusted servant to fetch *arrack*. Arrack, a liquor made from fermented rice and molasses, is forbidden in Iran, as is the opium heating in the brazier in the courtyard. The servant climbs down a stairway into an underground hideaway, a storage space for the ordinary sundries of the household. And there, carefully tucked behind firewood and burlap bags of rice, are small liquor barrels.

The arrack is strategically hidden. In the event of a raid, the servants dash up the same stairs and empty the barrels into the open pits of the outhouse.

In his zeal for modernization, Iran's new monarch, Reza Khan, the first of two Pahlavi monarchs, has condemned liquor and opium. He has declared that Iran is held back by the tradition of men idling away the days and nights puffing opium and consuming draughts of arrack. This behavior is anathema to the new Iran—backwards, indolent, and self-indulgent. The Shah formed the Mo'fatesh, a special police squad, to rid the country of opium and arrack.

The Mo'fatesh raid Mahmoud's compound regularly. There are no secrets in a small town. The surprise raids come swiftly, yet no search has yielded any contraband. Mahmoud is alternately amused and annoyed. He only hopes one of the frequent raids won't annoy his guests on this night, because it is a special one for Mahmoud.

The servant returns with a liquor barrel. Soghra pours the clear liquid into a hand-carved silver decanter and places it on a tray with shot glasses. She sends the servant out into the courtyard where Mahmoud sits with his guests. Sitting cross-legged on his carpet are the town's most educated, talented, and wealthiest men. Big-bellied men, they slap each other's backs and take their places in a circle. They let the weight of middle age and over indulgence sink into the floor cushions.

Twenty years ago these men were young renegades on the run. They hid in the hills above Kerman to escape being pressed into service in the British South Persian Rifles. Theirs is a brotherhood formed by shared danger.

Now they gather to talk politics, smoke opium, and drink arrack. They are nationalists who oppose both the monarch and the Islamic establishment. Their talk is laced with scorn and laughter for the politics of Iran. The Mo'fatesh is a joke to them. For hours their chatter will crisscross this circle. Occasionally, Mahmoud will raise his fist defiantly, evoking the passion of his father, Abolghassem.

The world has changed. The trans-Iranian railroad has reached Kerman, bringing with it new schools—a university in Tehran—new hospitals, and new factories by the hundreds. Yet despite Reza Khan's push toward modernity, the days and the pleasant nights seem the same as ever to these men.

Mahmoud is stoking the embers of the brazier, stirring up the heat. A hearty laugh erupts among the brotherhood.

Mahmoud calls to Reza: "*Pesar,* boy, bring my *taryak.*"

Reza knows this chore well. He shoves his chewed-up pencil into his textbook and scurries over to the water well on the other side of the courtyard. Feeling along the stone wall with his hand, he finds the chain and pulls up a sealed wooden case lined with zinc. Inside are rolls of opium. Reza takes a roll, reseals the case, and lowers it carefully into the well.

The goldfish in the wading pool zip away as he walks by. He spits at them flippantly.

Back at the edge of the circle on the carpet, Reza hands the opium stick to his father, who slips off the grease-proof paper and unties the cotton twine. With practiced skill, he cuts a pea-sized piece and sets it aside. The tiny bit is as black as the pupil of an eye. He then takes the *vafoor,* a pipe with a broad wooden tube attached to a tiny ceramic cup, and holds it over the fire. When the ceramic cup is hot enough, he spears the opium onto the chamber's roof with a thin metal spike. He then leans back on the cushion and, with a small pair of tongs, lifts a glowing ember to the cup until the opium juice begins to sizzle. Cupping the pipe, Mahmoud takes in a breath of the rich opium, holding it in his lungs as long as he can. He exhales leisurely through his nostrils; what the lungs did not absorb, the nose might take in. He passes the pipe, suppresses a cough, takes a swig from his tea, and chases it with a diamond-shaped piece of bakhlava.

Servants come and go. Trays of arrack, sweets, pistachios, and yogurt sit in the middle of the circle of men. The conversation hums on into the night. Mahmoud and his friends discuss the war and the Pahlavi king's mistakes in running the country during these economically depressed times. Sounding like politicians rather than merchants, they criticize the monarch desire for Iranians to be modern, like the Europeans, to shake off the fourteen-hundred-year-old culture of Islam.

Late into the night, stars sprinkle the night sky over Kerman. The desert air cools, and the men wrap wool cloaks around their shoulders. The opium smoke and laughter carry into the alleyways of the neighborhood. Across the courtyard, Javad has fallen asleep in Soghra's lap. She runs her fingers through his hair. She watches the servants clear the dinner plates. Soghra looks over at the men and sees that her husband will stay up late tonight.

In the morning, Mahmoud's family plans to board a bus for Mashad to visit Mahmoud's half-brother, Ahmad. Mahmoud and Ahmad have not spoken since 1920, when Abolghassem disinherited Ahmad and Mahmoud's other half-brother, Mehdy. Several months ago, Mahmoud breaks his father's wishes and delivers to Ahmad his share of the inheritance. That was his first olive branch. In Mashad, Mahmoud hopes to offer his second olive branch in another attempt to repair the relationship their father severed.

Soghra sees that Reza is falling asleep next to his father. Mahmoud shakes the boy gently, and Reza heads inside to sleep with the voices still murmuring in his ears.

The conversations slowly winds to an end. A quiet slumber falls over the house.

Just as dawn is about to break, right before roosters call and devout Muslims get up to pray, there is a sudden shriek from the courtyard. Reza and his sisters rush outside, wiping sleep from their eyes, presuming that Mo'fatesh officers have once again stormed the compound.

Soghra is bent over, beating her chest, wailing, damning the evil eye. Servants rush about. There are muffled voices and tears. Then the property gates open wide and a horse-drawn carriage rolls in. Reza sees the flash of white linen over the body as it is lifted onto the back of the wagon. His father Mahmoud is dead at age forty-eight.

When Abolghassem banishes his son Ahmad, he is disowned, wiped off the family scroll. To be the son of a second wife is bad enough, but to be disinherited? Soon after he is banished, Ahmad leaves Kerman. He goes to Mashad, a journey of several days to the northeast. It is as far as he could get from Kerman. It is also where the British give him work.

Later, when surnames become mandatory by law, Ahmad cannot take the Karbassi name. This infuriates him. Abolghassem's legacy is his renowned carpets, his land, the village of Kerman, and the name Karbassi. Ahmad is not a Karbassi. Even though Mahmoud graciously gives Ahmad his share of the inheritance, he cannot return Ahmad to the family. Ahmad lives with a scarred ego for the rest of his life.

Left to select his own family name, Ahmad takes on Shokoohi as his surname. Shokoohi means splendor. Magnificence. Dignity.

Ahmad has never reached out to Mahmoud, the first son of Abolghassem. But when he hears his half-brother has suddenly passed away, he takes the first bus back to Kerman.

When Ahmad arrives back in Kerman, it has been twenty years since his father disgraced him. But that was then. Now, he has rights. He is the eldest male member of the family. No one can dispute that.

He may be a member of the family by blood, but Ahmad is a stranger to all in the household. The servants usher him into the courtyard. The paisley print carpet is rolled out. Tea is poured from the samovar, fresh dates and pistachios are served.

Soghra vaguely recognizes him. She tightens her chador and sits on far edge of the carpet. She pulls the chador across her face and keeps her eyes away from him.

Ahmad takes a date and studies Soghra.

"*Khanom,* we are family. I am your husband's older brother. Nothing can change that. You may look at me."

"*Chashm Agha,*Yes, sir" but Soghra does not obey. She keeps her eyes down.

Ahmad picks up another date and contemplates the situation. There are four children who have never seen him before. The oldest is 13-year-old Reza. There are servants and carpet-makers. There are orchards.

"*Khanom,* if one wife is good, do you think two wives are better?"

"I don't know, sir."

"Do you think that you will make a good wife for me?"

"Why are you asking? I know my duty. I will obey."

"The Shah says that we are to educate our women now so that they can have opinions. Do you agree, *Khanom?* Do you have opinions?"

"May I speak, *Agha?*"

"Of course, I asked you for your opinions."

"I will be fine. And my family, we will be fine. I can read and write. We will manage."

"What are you saying—that you don't need me?"

She hesitates. "Yes, I am saying that."

"I offer to marry you, to protect you and your children, and you say no?"

Soghra tucks her chin into her chador.

"This is how educated women become—free to say no."

"I did not say no," Soghra replies. "I said that we don't need you. You have your right, I know that. But, I ask you . . ."

"You ask me? No, I will tell you. I have no use for a second wife. It's appalling and backward."

"Then you understand?"

"I understand that I don't need a second wife," Ahmad says. "But, I have decided—in the boy's best interest—that he will return with me to Mashad. Reza needs proper supervision."

"He is supervised here—he has no problems."

"No, a woman cannot raise a man."

"Please, no."

"You want him to become a man, don't you?

"He will learn here."

"He will work for me and learn from me."

"You want his inheritance—then I will give it to you—all of it—only leave my son with me."

"That is generous but beside the point. It is best for the boy. I will take him to Mashad in three days."

"You cannot! He is mine!"

"Don't argue with me, *Khanom*," Ahmad says. "I have made my decision."

"You only want the money coming to him from his father! You are greedy."

"Ha, I have money. I don't need more. I am only doing what my dear dead brother would want—a proper raising for a Karbassi boy."

"Give me my son or I will die."

The days pass in anguish for Soghra. She constantly begs and pleads with Ahmad.

On the third day, Ahmad summons Reza to say goodbye. Soghra's face is soaked with tears. Her voice is hoarse. She clutches Reza tightly to her bosom. Her heart pounds and her body heaves with sobs. She holds him for as long as she can.

Deeply frightened, Reza clings to his mother. Finally, Ahmad calls him, and the two walk away down the dusty alley to take a bus to Mashad.

In only a few days, Soghra loses her husband and her oldest son.

Chapter 7
Soghra

After rummaging through bundle after bundle of my parents'
photographs, a significant portion of them black-and-white
pictures of a bygone era, I find only three of my paternal
grandmother, Soghra. There's one in which she must have been
only four or five, standing next to her father, the cotton factory
owner. In another she is with her husband, my paternal
grandfather, Mahmoud. In this photo I also see my Aunt Aghdas,
then a toddler, now deceased, tucked between her parents,
Soghra and Mahmoud. Of the three photographs, the most
interesting is dated by the Farsi calendar as ١٤-١٢-١٣, which
corresponds to March 3, 1935.

The photograph intrigues me. From the vantage point of the
lens, I see a large group of Kermoonis; I count eighty, though I
might have missed a head or two. All the women are sitting in
the front rows, while their men stand behind. They are gathered
in some sort of courtyard. Persian carpets cover the stone floor,
and a large wading pool sits in the center, its water reflecting
many of the expectant faces staring into the camera. At the left
of the photograph, I spot my grandmother, Soghra. Oddly, she
and all the other women are wearing cloche hats and ankle-
length coats with collars—the iconic look of the Western world
during that era. Their faces look subdued.

Really subdued.

This photo was taken the day the women of Kerman, including my grandmother, were ordered to take off their chadors. The town's *ostandar,* governor, under orders from Reza Khan, was directed to photograph these women without their veils. I've read elsewhere that with this decree, the Pahlavi monarch wanted to prove to the Western world that Iran was shedding the traditions that he contended were holding it back from prosperity. Women's veils—a sign of their backwardness— were being stripped away to make way for the shah's modernizing agenda. Historians have written much about the connection between that period's unveiling and Iran's 1979 revolution, but I am not interested in those political analyses. I am curious to know more about my grandmother.

I search her tiny image for clues, seeking to understand her gaze. I ask the decomposing photograph: What was life like for you, Soghra, when you became a widow, as young as you were, with four children? How did you manage when your eldest son, my father, was taken away from you?

It's futile for me to seek answers from a photograph. The answers have vanished with the passage of time. All I do know is that Soghra's life was shadowed by sadness . . . right to the very end. And that tells me as much about my father as it does about her.

Kerman
1944

Soghra lies quarantined in a servant's room. She has infectious tuberculosis.

"Do not cross this line," Ahmad says. "You can stand here for a minute, but then back to the house. Is that clear?"

The four children nod. They are behind the threshold of the doorway, looking into the servant's room.

"You cannot enter this room—is that clear? If you go in, you will die."

Javad is crying.

"Stop crying! She doesn't need to see you crying like babies!"

This makes Javad cry louder.

"Enough! *Berin, berin,* from this doorway," Ahmad says. "Back to the house. Let her rest. Now go!"

Ahmad watches as his two nephews, Reza and Javad, and his two nieces, Soodabeh[3] and Aghdas, hurry away. He then steps to the threshold of the door to check on Soghra. He doesn't dare go in lest he catch the awful disease himself.

A month earlier, news of Soghra's illness brings Uncle Ahmad back to Kerman to take charge of family matters. He brings Reza along, not so much to make Soghra feel better but because Reza can help manage his siblings.

Four years have passed since Reza last saw his mother. He rushes to see her when they arrive, but he can come no closer than the doorway. Each day, Reza, his brother, and his sisters spend as much time as Ahmad allows, kneeling at the doorway looking into the room.

It is a barren room that stinks with disease. There are no windows, and what light exists seeps through the doorway, casting ominous shadows. As his eyes adjust from the bright desert light to the dark, Reza begins to see his mother.

---

[3] Soodabeh is a pseudonym to avoid confusion. My father's youngest sister is also named Akhtar.

Her hair is wildly disheveled. She is gaunt, her cheeks are sallow. A hand gropes out from the bedding, searching for a glass of water. Then her body convulses fiercely in a painful tubercular cough.

"*Janam,*" Soghra says, wincing in pain. "Javad *joon,* my dear."

"Moman," Javad whines. Soghra buries her face in her palms to weep, her cough becoming more violent.

"Moman," Javad pleads again, his voice drowned out by her coughing. Javad moves toward her. Reza holds him back.

"Come on, Javad, let's let her sleep. We will see her again soon," Reza says. "Let's go before Uncle comes back. Do you want to kick the ball with me?"

They peel themselves away and head back to the main compound. Reza, still holding Javad's hand, fights back his own tears.

Reza is twice the size of Javad: they look like father and son as they walk side-by-side toward the main building. Reza still hears his mother's cough. The large wading pool is cloudy, thick with moss and algae. One goldfish mouths the slimy water where Reza spit the day his father died.

Reza forces a smile, tousles his brother's short hair, and gently claps him on his back, "Javad, get a soccer ball."

Each day, Reza and his siblings return from school to their vigil at the door of their mother's room. One day they arrive to find the room empty. For a second, Reza thinks their mother has recuperated and will emerge to embrace them, that her bedding has been rolled up because the quarantine is over. But Soghra never appears, and the four of them kneel by her door until Uncle Ahmad comes to fetch them.

Reza is now seventeen. Whenever he feels a deep longing for home, he fights it off, banishes those feelings. If he let the vine of homesickness start to grow, it would swallow him whole. Now he is home, and yet he feels homeless. The courtyard is as familiar to him as his hand, but the wading pool is thick with the sludge of neglect. The pots still simmer in the kitchen, but the once happy sounds of women cooking together are now somber murmurs.

Sometimes Reza ducks out of the compound and walks through the alleys outside. He wanders aimlessly until he finds himself beneath the oak tree of the mosque, Masjid Malik. In better days, he and his mother would serve food to the poor during the mourning period of Imam Husayn. He thinks of the last procession of the *nazr*—they carried twelve candles, each his height. "How high would the candles have to be today?" he wonders.

Returning to the compound, Reza slips in through a servants' entrance, passing the house where his mother died. He stops by the open door of the kitchen. The warm smell of bread baking in the wood-fired oven reaches him. He watches the bread woman pound and fold the dough for tomorrow's bread. She is strong and steady—pound and fold, then pound and fold again.

Reza steps into the kitchen. He begins to pound, fold, and roll the dough for no reason. The bread woman steps back. He is pounding on the dough—harder and harder—tears rolling down his face.

The next day, Reza is sitting on the carpet in the courtyard with his uncle. Uncle Ahmad announces that it is time to leave for Mashad. In four years, Reza has grown to equal his father's height.

"God help me," Ahmad says. "Four children—four times the burden—I could at least have four children who help—not these limp, crying, wet dishrags."

But now, sitting in the courtyard where his father had died, Reza watches his brother and sisters with a different eye. Who will care for Javad, who carries his grief like a mortal injury? Who will care for Soodabeh and Aghdas?

"Uncle Ahmad," Reza asks, "will we all go to Mashad tomorrow?"

"No. You and I will go, and we will send for the others later."

"Who will care for them?"

"The servants are here, and the girls can feed the boy. It's past time they learn."

"Maybe we should wait to see if they can manage."

"Wait? No, I can't stand it here anymore. It's cursed—a house of death. Even the goldfish is dead. No, we leave first thing in the morning, so pack your sack tonight."

"What will happen to father's house?"

"I have to study that—but in time we will close it up and sell it."

"I am seventeen, Uncle."

"What is that supposed to mean?"

"I will stay here."

"No, you won't do that. There's no point."

"I am the oldest in my family. It is my duty to take care of," he pauses to swallow a lump in his throat, "all of this and Javad, Soodabeh, and Aghdas. They need me."

Ahmad turns to look at his nephew who meets his gaze directly.

"You're still a boy."

"No, I am the oldest. I will stay here and do my duty."

"You don't know what duty is, you don't know what it means to be responsible."

"You don't know any more than I do. But the first step is knowing your duty and stepping forward to accept it."

"Big talk from a little man."

"I am as tall as you are."

"God help me—you are a Karbassi through and through. Stubborn. Were you all born thinking that you were never wrong? I should put you on the ass of an ass and send you to Bandar Abbas."

Reza stands.

"Sit down, Reza, sit down. I won't bother. And that's what you are—all of you—too much bother. So have your little manhood game. You can have your little boys and girls to take care of."

"Thank you, sir."

"Tomorrow I will be on the bus to Mashad. If I were you, I would be on that bus with me. In Mashad, I can help you. If you are here, well . . . you are here. So, sleep on it *pesar*."

"I will, sir. I will think it over."

Reza turns to walk away.

"Boy, mark my words: this is a house of death. Do you hear me?"

Life in the compound continues. The servants continue to cook meals and sweep the courtyard. The two girls still huddle together to play their games. Occasionally Reza kicks the ball around with Javad, but he most often sits on the paisley carpet in the courtyard doing nothing.

There is nothing to worry about. Their father has left a seemingly endless supply of money. Reza is seeing that the others are fed. He makes sure Javad goes to school.

But life is not the same in their hearts. Reza feels a dark cloud pressing down on him, smothering him. He hides his deep depression from the others. He is the oldest; he must be strong. One look at Javad's face feels like a kick in the stomach. Javad, who still cries at night, looks lost, with empty eyes and hollow cheeks.

Reza feels chained to the carpet where he sits every day. "I am thinking," he tells himself. Once he can think things through, he will know what to do. He should work with the carpet weavers—take over the family business. But death has played a cruel trick on him beyond the loss of his parents. Growing up in Kerman, Reza assumed he would learn the business—how to design, weave, and sell the Karbassi carpets. He would learn to graft the pistachio trees, to heft a peach and judge its readiness for the market. He would learn how to trade in land, to recognize the most fertile soil, and acquire access to water. Instead, at age thirteen, Reza was taken away to a school in Mashad to be groomed to marry his cousin, Ahmad's daughter. In Mashad, he learned math and history.

Should go back to school? he wonders.

He is aware that the servants are watching him. When he looks back, their eyes dart away. He doesn't know what to do, but he fears showing weakness. Relatives, neighbors, and friends visit the children, bringing little gifts and treats. Reza assures them that all is fine.

And so, the days plod on. The pistachio harvest is meager that year. When the gardener nonchalantly tells him so, Reza tries to upbraid him.

"We must do better," he says, trying to imagine how his father would sound. The gardener just stares at him, then laughs and walks away. The off-year harvest is always light.

In the spring, one gardener leaves. Soon the apprentice weavers leave to work for another family. The room where his mother died remains empty—a permanent quarantine.

Shortly before the anniversary of his mother's death, Javad comes down with a high fever. Reza calls a doctor. "Wash his feet in cold water," he is told. The fever lingers. The visiting relatives are unconcerned: it's just another sign of the poor boy's deep grief. "He will get better in time," they assure Reza.

For three days and two nights, his sisters cool Javad down with wet rags. Reza stands vigil by his younger brother's side. By the third night, Javad's skin, already chalky white, burns with a vengeance. "God help me," Reza prays. He puts his bedding by Javad's and holds his brother's hand tightly. Maybe through his hand he can guide his deep love into Javad, maybe he can pull him back from the fever. Throughout the night, his brother's hand seems to get colder with each passing hour.

Sinking into sleep, still holding Javad's hand tightly, Reza dreams about their mother: Soghra is holding Javad as she did when he was a toddler, with her hip shifted to the side. Javad is running his hands through her hair. They both smile at him— radiant smiles that felt warm in the cool night.

Reza awakens fresh from the dream. He thinks, "Everything's all right now." Javad's hand, still locked in his, is as cold as ice. For a brief moment he thinks the fever has broken.

Then it dawns on him: Javad is dead. Reza closes his eyes. He imagines he can see his mother and Javad hugging. He wants to call to them, "Take me with you, Moman, take *me* with you!"

Reza opens his eyes. Javad's body is still. Reza's heart is empty. It is as if it has been turned off, never to start up again.

"Javad *joon*," Reza says softly to his brother's listless body. "My life, you have taken my life with you."

Reza looks down at Javad's hand still clutching his. He begins to pry the fingers off so he can get up and tell his sisters. He thinks, "If only I could pull Javad back from the other side. If only . . ."

Chapter 8
Brother

If my Uncle Javad were alive today, he would be seventy-two years old.

While writing this family history, I gave Baba one of my early drafts to read. He sobbed when he got to the part I had written about his brother. His shoulders shook and tears streamed from under his bifocals. Between each page he flipped, he took in deep breaths. I was surprised that he didn't stop to correct my errors, a wrong date or name of a relative. He read through his brother's story without stopping. He'd blow his nose and then continue. Rarely had I seen my father shed a tear. Who knew this ache, like a parasite, lived in him? A raw pain he had learned to cover with his angry demeanor. Watching Baba read his brother's story was an eye-opening experience for me. For the first time, I really *saw* my father.

Now when I look at Baba, I see how Javad's passing, more than anything else, has shaped his character. Losing his brother was a proverbial catalyst that shaped the husband and father he was to become. As you read more of our family tale, you might disagree. You may see other events in my father's life that shaped the man he is. But I will disagree. Because, you see, I too can claim to know the pain of losing a brother.

**Narragansett
2005**

Akhtar balances a carton under one arm, holding the stair rail with the other. At the bottom of the steps, on the landing leading to the garage, she has set up an assembly line of boxes. They hold the sum of their life: a Russian nesting doll that Reza brought back in 1970 after his assignment in Russia; the baseball cap she earned for being a model employee at the Stop & Shop in Wakefield; unopened lotions and soaps she got as gifts, which she always thought would be a shame to waste on herself; a large bag of matchbooks Reza used to collect when he and his NIOC colleagues went to lunch or dinner in New York City, and so on. A jumble of unsorted, unsortable junk that will soon meet its eventual destination: garbage, charity, one of her three children, or Iran.

The pile of things going to Iran is the smallest. Heavy items can't go—too expensive to ship. And some memories are still dangerous. Reza's picture with the Shah will have to stay here.

The process drains her emotionally. Each piece of clothing, each box of papers, each child's creation demands her attention. Each opens a door into a long hallway of memories, where Akhtar feels compelled to go. By trying to assemble every piece of memory into a whole, maybe she can finally understand. While she searches every item for answers, redemption, or reconciliation, Reza seems to be unaffected by the sorting process.

From where she's standing at the end of the hallway, holding a box under her bosom, she watches Reza in his threadbare yellow chair. She can only see a part of her husband's back, with his head bent down. His gray hair is disheveled. From the back he seems softer, not the angry man she has seen too often. It stirs her compassion, almost pity, for her husband.

He looks about ready to drop another folder into the trash. Knowing her husband's unsentimental ways, she thinks the garbage pail she has set by his chair is not nearly large enough.

Moving on toward her own pile of work, she picks up a cardboard box, on the side of which is the name of her middle child, her son Kambiz, scrawled in Farsi. The Farsi script looks like a bird in flight, its wings high up, soaring through the sky, far away from its nest. Of her three children, Kambiz flew the farthest from the coop. And yet he lives the closest to them—just one town over.

Kambiz is a mirror image of Reza when he was young. He has the same deep dark eyes, downturned lips, and slender, straight nose.

From a paper shopping bag, she pulls out a meticulously cut and laminated newspaper clipping from a 1976 *Saunderstown Herald,* the local newspaper. In the center of the clipping is a photograph of Kambiz, young and handsome.

* * *

It is May 1976—a few weeks before America burst with bicentennial patriotism. Kambiz comes home right from school and sits down at the kitchen table. Akhtar scurries to fix him a snack. Kambiz takes his time.

"Not hungry," he says.

"Azizam? What is it?" A 17-year-old boy is always hungry. Still, the dates remain untouched.

"Nothing."

Akhtar begins to make tea, boiling water on the stove, arranging the glass beakers, spooning the tea leaves into the teapot. They sit in silence at the oval table—tea steeping and Kambiz thinking. Akhtar searches for the right thing to say. Kambiz has created a shell around himself. He has had that shell for as long as she can remember.

"Is it school, Kambiz-joon?" she asks, worried that her question might provoke him to leave the kitchen so he can avoid talking.

"It's nothing." But, he stays put.

The kitchen is rich with the smell of fresh-baked bread—the smell of home, here and in Iran. It is the smell of her grandmother—Jan-Bibi. Akhtar opens the oven, gingerly removing a loaf. She should let it stand, but she pulls out a bread knife and slices a piece for Kambiz. It folds and melts onto the plate. Kambiz slips it into his mouth. Akhtar cuts another piece.

"Is it your grades? You always get good grades."

"Yes, I do," he says fiercely. "I always get good grades, don't I?"

"Yes you do. You're one of the best."

"Moman, I am the best."

"Of course, you are the best because you work as hard as you can."

"No, I am the best in school. I have the best score of anyone."

"Kambiz! Don't tease me."

"It's true. The principal told me."

"Then you will get a prize, right?"

Kambiz takes a swallow of tea.

"Your father—he will be so proud of you—the best grades—in an American school! And a prize."

"No."

"It's everything he's wanted—an education cannot be taken away from you."

"There's no prize."

"But, the principal said you are the best."

"He said there must be some kind of a mistake."

"Mistake?"

"I'm a 'foreigner.' A 'foreigner' can't be valedictorian. The principal said he had to do a recount. They're questioning it ... saying, how can a foreigner out-perform their own students. So they are deciding whether a 'foreigner' can be the Valedictorian."

To Akhtar the word valedictorian sounds brave, like the legendary valiant Persian hero, Rostam, at the highest peak of the Damavand Mountains outside Tehran. Kambiz too is at the top, but no one can see him there.

Kambiz's high school graduation.

Akhtar remembers the deep green school lawn on that spring afternoon, reminiscent of the lush lawn in the photograph Khan Daee sent to Tehran. In the sunlight, the stunning green carpet spread under the rows of white chairs and then stretched out behind the high school. Akhtar, Reza, and Kambiz's younger sister come early to get front-row seats. They are dressed formally: Akhtar with high heels and handbag, Reza in a three-piece suit. Maybe they are overdressed. But, she doesn't care. They are dressed to honor Reza's dream—an American education. Now Kambiz is half-way there and, like Rostam before him, at the top of the heap. She and Reza feel as if they are floating on a magic carpet of green.

Kambiz Karbassi is introduced as the class valedictorian.

And there is Kambiz striding to the podium, his brown graduation robe trailing behind him. There he is towering over the podium—standing more than six feet tall, a boy no more. Reza is ecstatic— beaming like a beacon and clapping wildly for his son. Akhtar feels tears welling in her eyes. Here is her child—whose first language is Farsi, whose grandfather could not read or write—standing before hundreds of Americans eager to listen to his words. Here is her child who had weathered taunts and sneers from his classmates. Now they must hear from him.

Then, Kambiz is speaking into the microphone. Akhtar feels as though she is watching a silent movie—her beautiful son speaking this foreign tongue, speaking from his heart. The words seem to flow over her. Then she catches one word—Persia. Home. Kambiz states that his goal in life is to return home to Persia. To Iran, thinks Akhtar, to Sadegh and Tayebeh. To a world of friends and family. To home.

* * *

She looks down at the newspaper clipping still in her hand. The headline reads, "This Year's Senior Valedictorian." It tells a rosy, even rousing story of Kambiz. It describes how her son comes to this country with his parents and siblings, how in a short period of time he learns English and excels in school, and how he plans to go back to his homeland after he finishes college. There it is, she thinks, written proof.

Akhtar is glad they laminated it to preserve it. Maybe one day Kambiz's two kids will want to read about their father, about the fact that his greatest dream was to return home to Iran. She rolls up the article and tucks it back into the box. She seals the box with packing tape. It is ready for Kambiz to pick up during his next visit, which, she sadly notes, is rare. She traces his name in Farsi on the outside of the box, letting her finger soar along the wings of his name.

She lifts two cartons and carries them to the garage. The humid July morning makes her perspire. She plunks the boxes at her feet. The garage is in disarray. She straightens her back, feeling the ache of old age. Wiping her brow with the back of one hand and grabbing the handle of a garbage can with the other, she begins to pull. She drags the bin from one side of the garage to the other. Its tin bottom scrapes against the concrete, a screeching noise that unsettles her nerves. She is still thinking of Kambiz.

Sometimes she feels that she is in a dark theater watching a movie of Kambiz in her memory. There he is starting college. Kambiz follows in his brother's footsteps: he chooses to study engineering at the University of Rhode Island. In Iran, an engineer earns the title of *Mohandes,* equivalent in prestige to the title of doctor. He would be *Mohandes* Karbassi, a scholar who knows how machines and buildings work, just as a doctor knows how the body works.

Kambiz goes through high school without friends. But at the university he meets a small group of young Iranian students, ten or twelve young people who have been sent to the States by their parents to achieve the same goals that had possessed Reza: to earn that dazzling American education credential. Shah Reza

Pahlavi, like his father before him, is pushing to modernize Iran and the country is booming with development. Engineering promises good pay and prestige in Iran. All of Kambiz's new Iranian friends are enrolled in engineering. "Mohandes Karbassi" must have sounded good to him, holding the promise of a prosperous future.

Kambiz is welcomed into this circle of friends. But it is a friendship born out of a certain time and place. In Iran, these boys would have never socialized with the son of a bureaucrat. They are the sons of the Shah's elite, living extravagantly in the U.S. and are supported by endless blank checks from their families in Tehran.

They are a clean-shaven bunch who drove expensive sports cars and wear designer clothing and gold watches. They had all gone to private boarding schools in Europe. When they are not in their houses in Narragansett or Kingston—paid for with cash, of course—they are on the beach in the south of France or shopping in Paris.

In America, though, class lines have a way of blurring. Kambiz is accepted into the group, even though he typically wears nothing more extravagant than faded jeans and t-shirts and drives a rusty orange Chevette—paid for with the money his grades earned him under the Shah's scholarship fund. Kambiz finds a home with his new friends. He breaks out of his shell and now laughs readily, clearly eager to become *Mohandes* Karbassi.

The movie reel spins forward—to 1981. Kambiz's dream of returning to Iran, like his father's, is on hold. He has earned his graduate degree from Purdue University and is living at home while he searches for a job. The orange Chevette, dented now, pulls into the driveway. Kambiz is home from another job interview.

The engine sputters to a stop. Akhtar watches through the vestibule window as Kambiz lets his head droop to the steering wheel. He sits like that for quite a while before coming into the house. Akhtar has already placed the water on the stove for tea.

Kambiz takes his seat at the oval table. Before he says a word, Akhtar knows. He has been rejected again.

"Today they asked," Kambiz says. "As if my name doesn't say it enough."

"What did they ask?"

"My nationality."

"What did you say?"

"Iranian. I can't lie. Look at me. Everything about me screams 'Iranian.' My skin, my hair, my eyes. My god damn name!"

Akhtar sips her tea.

Kambiz continues, "Straight A's through college, honor rolls, awards, and what does it come down to—what is your nationality?"

Akhtar clears his lunch plate, serving him another beaker of tea. Reza brings in the mail. There is a letter for Kambiz. Another rejection, he is sure.

"Open it," Reza says.

Kambiz leaves it on the table.

"Well? What are you waiting for?"

Kambiz opens it, skims it, and tosses it onto the floor.

"No, not another one," Akhtar says.

"No, it's not another one."

"A job! That's great. Congratulations," Reza comments incredulously but happily. He retrieves the letter from the floor. "It *is* a job. They want you to start next month."

"Look at it again, Baba."

He reads it again. "What?"

"It's not a job. It's an insult."

"A job is a job. They want you to work for them, boy."

"Entry level."

"So what? It's pay."

"I have a master's degree. I was the best in the class. Do you think I should sweep floors for them?"

"It's an engineering job."

"Maybe I can hold the door for the boss when he comes through."

"You will prove yourself. Work your way up. Like I did."

"Work your way up? Boosted up by your uncle."

"Boosted up? What the hell do you know? I worked for everything I got."

"I don't see any fancy cars coming in here to help me."

"You are ungrateful. I have given you everything. An education in America. You should be on top of the world."

"Education in America? Education, education, that's all I hear from you. I got your damned education in America and Americans don't want me."

"You got an education—finest in the world. Now, it's up to you to work your ass off."

"You mean lick their boots so I can take out their trash."

"You're not good enough."

"Good enough? How would you know? I am the best: honor roll, straight A student, dean's list, cum laude. You think all that was easy?"

"You're afraid to work. No one's going to hand you money like your rich college friends."

"Reza, please," Akhtar jumps in.

"Reza, please? shut up Khanom. I worked to give this ungrateful dog everything."

"Admit it—it's a lie—education means nothing—nothing."

"That's enough out of you."

"It means shit, and you don't know because you're hiding— hiding in your little room, listening to your damn radio. You think that radio from Tehran will tell you what the world is like. Wake up, blind man! It's who you know and what color your skin is."

"Get out! Get out of my house."

"Reza!"

"It's my house, damn it. I'll put the dog out myself."

Reza charges towards Kambiz. Kambiz dodges him. Akhtar rushes between them. She collides with Reza.

"Both of you stop, for God's sake," Akhtar says, clutching Reza by his shirt.

"That's all right, Moman. I get the picture. I'm not good enough for you."

Kambiz calmly walks out the door. Akhtar hears the Chevette struggle to start and then sputter to life. In a moment, it is gone.

Emrika-e.

In July 1993, Kambiz marries Elizabeth, an *emrika-e* with blonde hair and blue eyes. Not the beautiful raven black of Persian women, not even a soulful brown. Elizabeth is emrika-e, a word that conjures difference, foreignness, otherness.

Reza and Akhtar drive to Connecticut for the wedding. They watch the Christian wedding ceremony. There is Kambiz, standing straight-backed before the pastor. Beside him stood Elizabeth in an elegant white wedding dress.

Reza and Akhtar stand when the audience stand, but they feel lost.

The pastor asks Kambiz and Elizabeth if they agree to be wed. Each answered in turn, "I do."

Akhtar glances over at Reza, who is standing as tall and straight as his son. "I poured the beaker of tea," she thinks to herself. "I never said 'I do'—I obeyed."

The reception is at a country club. There is a swirl of flashy colors: bright preppy clothes, checkered pants, and raspberry Izod shirts. The string trio playing a waltz is nearly drowned out by the happy buzz of the guests as they mingle, cocktails in their hands.

In the center of it all is Kambiz, sharing a laugh, tossing down a drink, shaking hands with guests. There is Kambiz throwing his arm around his new father-in-law, laughing with him at some inside joke.

Akhtar and Reza barely move from their secure spot by the wall. She is not sure what they should do. Reza squirms impatiently. Finally, they leave quietly. They are foreigners.

Kambiz and Elizabeth now live about a fifteen-minute drive from them. Kambiz has done well running his own construction company. He has jumped from a Chevette to a BMW. He owns a modern, spacious home at the end of a long driveway that winds through several acres of lawn and trees. It's a house Kambiz wishes he could proudly show off to his rich Iranian college friends, but they no longer keep in touch.

The last time Akhtar and Reza visited Kambiz and Elizabeth is a year earlier.

Akhtar is sitting in their chic living room on a white leather couch. At her feet is a dog, large and black, panting and drooling on the Persian rug that Reza had given to Kambiz. Every few minutes, the dog slurps loudly.

Kambiz pours a glass of beer for Reza and sets it on a coaster on the glass coffee table.

He speaks to them in English. It would be rude to speak Farsi to them in front of Elizabeth. His English words sound cold. Akhtar feels like she is listening to a stranger.

Reza says to Kambiz, "Did you hear about this Ahmadinejad guy who wants to run for president? *Iran Times* did a story on him this month. He looks like a monkey. He'll never win."

Kambiz nods his head, not really listening.

"Well, do you know who I am talking about?"

Akhtar remembers how some time ago, before Kambiz met Elizabeth, her son used to be interested in Iran's politics. During those early days of the Revolution, he and Reza would sit at the oval kitchen table listening to the shortwave radio. That was until the disappointments came, before Kambiz was looking for jobs and being rejected. After that, he seemed to care less about Iran.

"Baba, I've got a business to worry about. Who cares who this guy is?"

Akhtar clasps her hands on her lap. She peers toward the kitchen where she can hear the meal being prepared. Her offer to help has been politely refused. From the game room she can hear grandchildren lost in play. She wishes they spoke Farsi so that she could speak to them from her heart.

Reza takes a sip from his beer and smiles at his grandchildren, now in sight in the other room. That's about the extent of the affection he shows for them. A smile and a pat on the head. Reza shows little warmth towards his grandchildren save his youngest grandchild, his daughter's daughter, Donya. On the day she was born, Reza said, "She has my mother's eyes."

But Akhtar longs to touch and be with all her grandchildren, to be to them what Jan-Bibi had been to her. Instead she is confined to the white leather couch, guarded by a drooling dog.

In the dining room, Elizabeth proudly serves fish for dinner. Other than small talk, little is said among them. Reza's fork rattles against his plate adding to the uneasy quiet. Akhtar fiddles with her meal and smiles gamely.

Finally, the dinner is over. She is relieved. Akhtar stands to help clear the table and do the dishes. Kambiz ushers her back into her seat. She sits helplessly, watching through the door as Elizabeth begins the dishes. The dog trots right into the kitchen, its tongue lolling out of its mouth. Elizabeth holds a plate before the dog and the big tongue laps hungrily at the plate.

Sadegh, her religious father, would never have allowed a dog to enter the house. No soap could purify a plate licked by a dog. *Pedar saag,* son of a dog, is an insult in Iran. Akhtar is filled with revulsion and shame.

In the kitchen, the dog wags its tail gleefully. Akhtar sits at the dining room table.
Emrika-e.

That dinner was a year ago. She and Reza have not been invited back, Akhtar thinks, as she returns to her sorting in the garage. Deep in a box there is a pocket-sized photograph of an 18-month-old baby, plump, with a shy smile. She thinks about the very first time she saw this photograph. She was living in

London, three thousand miles away from Kambiz. Her father had carried Kambiz to a photographer's shop in Kerman. He had propped the little boy up to pose for this single photo to send to Akhtar.

Bringing the photograph close to her face, she wishes she could still smell her

son's baby scent. She remembers how, during those precious, tender years when a child should nestle into a mother's bosom and be forming an inseparable bond, she wasn't with Kambiz. She wasn't there when his first tooth came in, nor was she there when he took his first step. She holds the photograph close to her chest, as though she wants to cradle and croon to him as she never did back then.

Sitting in London, she would trace all the shadows and lines of this black-and-white photograph. How she yearned for Kambiz, how she cried every night. She would study his face, his eyes, his little hands, his mop of black hair. She tried to imagine how he sounded. She thinks about the hours she spent with this photograph. It was like a life raft that kept her afloat those three years in London. She wonders, what had little Kambiz felt for his mother in those years? The photograph brings back the pain of their separation. Kambiz's baby image stares back innocently. A tear rolls down Akhtar's cheek. She realizes that her guilt has never died, no matter how deep she's tried to bury it.

Chapter 9
Kambiz

While we were growing up, Kambiz and I were like any brother and sister. We teased and poked at each other, laughed and annoyed one another. He once tried to flush me down the toilet. I relate that story to my children these days, and I still manage to laugh when picturing the scene: how he dangled my head over the toilet bowl because I had played a practical joke on him. Kambiz was the typical Iranian brother, whose family charge was to take care of (or rather, watch over) his younger sister. I remember him as the person I'd run to if I had a nightmare—I never dared to go inside my parents' bedroom. I remember him tutoring me on my schoolwork and passing along some of the best books I've ever read: *Catcher in the Rye, 1984, To Kill a Mockingbird, The Child Buyer.* And in my teens, if Baba ever allowed me to attend a party, Kambiz was my chaperone.

But these days, Kambiz doesn't speak to me. We haven't spoken since we were in our twenties. My children have never seen their *daee,* their uncle.

I believe Kambiz has changed. I liken him to Richard Rodriguez, the Mexican American author who writes eloquently about being estranged from his culture and his family. Kambiz fills that role in our family: the successful, fully assimilated American who has little empathy for the culture he has shed.

Kambiz's story has been the most difficult for me to write about. During the process, I've experienced much more emotion than I bargained for, often more than I could process. When you write about a brother you've lost, it's like digging for a lost bond. You till dead soil, turning it over and over as you look for answers. In the muck you deal with, you plant seeds of doubt. Finally, you reap regret. In trying to portray Kambiz's role in our family, I've had to struggle to understand certain events. I've wondered how much of it has been fate, how much of it *choice*. In the end, writing about my lost brother has allowed me to comprehend deeper connections with our family roots—connections that explain why Kambiz and I had a doomed relationship right from the very start.

In 1998, Kambiz became a father. He and his daughter, Sabine, share the same birthday: January 7. They also share Kambiz's olive skin. Sabine, a Latin name, means optimist. I was not surprised Kambiz would give his daughter a name that reflects Western culture. What I was shocked by—and admittedly even heartbroken about—was that Kambiz gave up his paternal name. He gave Sabine his wife's surname.

I find it ironic that Abolghassem denied two of his sons the Karbassi name, and then three generations later his great-grandson—the blood of his favored son—rejected his lineage. I also think how different Kambiz and I have turned out to be. He has tried to wipe himself clear of the very same family legacy that I am trying to preserve.

Oh, the twists and ironies—and sometimes parallels—of our family history . . .

Kerman
1946

Over one thousand years ago, the Persian poet Ferdowsi chronicled the rich traditions of Persian mythology in the Shahnameh, the Book of Kings. Hailed as the guardian of Farsi, Ferdowsi's stories are written in poetic form and in the old language. The book contains over 60,000 verses of poetry based on pre-Islamic folklore and history, and is regaled as one of Iran's most popular and influential national epics.

Of the numerous stories in the Shahnameh, the mythical character Rostam is perhaps the most celebrated. This titan, this champion of champions, is splendid in both strength and courage. In one tale, the child Rostam slays the maddened white elephant of King Manuchehr and tames his legendary stallion, Rakhsh. In a hero's journey "Rostam's Seven Quests," he sets out to save his sovereign, Kay Kavus, who was captured by the demons of Mazandaran. While Rostam
serves capricious kings, his true allegiance is to the greater good of his nation's people.

The story that is the most popular, and of course the most tragic, is the one in which Rostam unknowingly kills his son, Sohrab. While in battle, mighty Rostam slays Sohrab with a sword. He then stands over his victim, feeling like a victor, and the two exchange words. It is in that final moment of Sohrab's life that Rostam realizes they are father and son.

* * *

"She's only fourteen," Aunt Nosrat said to Reza emphatically. "Don't clip her wings." That was yesterday.

In the palm of his hand, Reza is holding a handful of pebbles. From time to time, he flips one up into the air. Reza, now nineteen, is sitting on the sun-faded carpet in the courtyard, deep in thought. From across the courtyard he can hear the drone of his two sisters chatting in the kitchen. They are peeling onions for the midday meal. They sit on wooden crates, their long black dresses drooping to the ground.

Reza picks up a pebble from his hand and tosses it toward the abandoned servants' house. He spies a plastic ball at the edge of the water pump—right where Javad left it over a year ago. Reza wings a pebble toward the ball. He misses. Next he aims for a dead jasmine bush—dead from neglect, since the gardeners have gone. He flicks a pebble into the old wading pool, now full of slimy moss.

"These are the boundaries of my world," he thinks. "From here to the compound walls, anything I can hit with a rock."

He throws another pebble right at the old wooden front gate. It makes a hollow thud. He used to like the gate. Behind it were surprises—usually the unexpected visits of relatives.

He throws another pebble. He hits the wooden door again. Now the outside world seems to be reaching in to invade the little world he has created with his sisters.

Yesterday, Aunt Nosrat dropped by. Aunt Nosrat is Abolghassem's stepdaughter, the daughter of the widow Abolghassem took for his second wife. She has become a regular visitor to this unusual family of three. Aunt Esmat, Abolghassem's oldest daughter by his first wife, the three's closest blood relative, never comes. She is strictly religious and confines herself to her house.

While Aunt Esmat retreats from the world in observant faith, Aunt Nosrat is sturdy and defiant. Like Abolghassem, she blazes her own trail without a care for the opinions of the world. Her marriage to a man half her age is considered a scandal in Kerman. She pursued her education, finished high school, and now serves as principal of the girls' high school. She is employed while other women stay home. She is publicly active in a society where women are expected to obey. She seeks freedom for women. Reza's Aunt Esmat scorns her half-sister, tells Nosrat that she should stop associating with the British in Kerman. Their values have made her sister a loose woman, she says. But like her brothers Ahmad and Mehdy, Nosrat seems to gravitate toward the British, to their way of life. Something pulls at her to emulate them.

Aunt Nosrat often comes by to cheer up Reza and his sisters. She brings them little gifts that are designed to teach. She brings them books and sparks their desire to read by pointing out the intriguing parts. She brings them a pencil or a fountain pen. She brings them jars of ink in many colors. She brings them paper. Once she brought Reza a stylish notebook. But yesterday she came empty handed. She came only to deliver a piece of news.

When Aunt Nosrat learned that the merchant Agha Ahmad was intending to ask for the hand of Reza's younger sister, Aghdas, she went directly to Reza. She did not want men to decide the fate of her stepniece. She did not want Aghdas to be bartered and traded like a sheep or goat.

Reza was stunned. His baby sister marrying someone?

Aunt Nosrat told him, "As the head of household and guardian of Aghdas, it is your responsibility to decide. You, Reza, must decide not only whom she will marry but when."

Reza glanced across the courtyard where he could see his sisters' heads bowed together, locked in conversation. Aghdas and Soodebeh are inseparable.

Aunt Nosrat came straight to the point. "Aghdas is too young for marriage," she said, and she laid out the facts of the matter:

Agha Ahmad is more than twice his sister's age. He is a well-established merchant. He lives with his mother and brother. Certainly, the family has a good reputation in Kerman. However, Agha Ahmad is only one of two surviving children. His mother, Robabeh, has buried seven children, which has made her into a cold, hardhearted woman. She is tender with her sons. But, Aunt Nosrat warned Reza, as the young bride and newcomer to the house, Aghdas will be treated like a servant—maybe worse.

Now, Reza alone will have to decide his sister's fate. Aunt Nosrat made strong points to dissuade Reza from letting her marry. Since then, Reza has been consumed by the question. Sitting in the corner of the courtyard, he tosses the stones in his palm into the air as he thinks. The stones fall back into his hand and he throws them again into the air. He is juggling three lives. Soodabeh will be lonely. Aghdas may be unhappy. He feels alone, uncertain, and trapped.

Yet he finds the other side of the case equally convincing. Aghdas will have financial security with this older man. If she stays, he thinks, he is not sure how he can guarantee that she will eat every day. To give Aghdas away would at least lessen the burden he's had to carry.

Across the courtyard, his sisters have their heads together over a cooking pot. To tear them apart will be difficult. Reza tries to imagine what it means to be a husband. Then it occurs to him: Agha Ahmad is old enough to be his father.

He toys with the rocks in his hand and flings them up once more. This time he lets them fall.

A month later, Aghdas is settled in the house of her new husband. Reza does not feel relieved by his decision. He consoles himself with the thought that the marriage was an economic necessity for the family. The inheritance is almost gone. He has sold all but a few of the remaining carpets. What will he do if they run out of money? Beg from his relatives? No, he cannot even consider that.

He has taken to pacing round and round the fetid wading pool. He still tosses pebbles. He now can hit the plastic ball still wedged by the water pump. He can thump the front gate with a good shot.

Then December comes. Reza hears a car honking right outside the front gate. He struggles to open the heavy doors. There is a crowd gathered around a big car that is rumbling slowly over the unpaved rocky path. Everybody is curious— there is a car in the Masjid Malik neighborhood! There is only one car in all of Kerman, a noisy clunker owned by the wealthy Jamshid Khan. But his car is a lame donkey compared to the shiny stallion coming up the path.

The car halts in front of the Karbassi gates. The crowd steps back as the chauffer—wearing cap and uniform—hustles to open the back door. Before he can open it, a thin man with broad shoulders steps out nimbly. He looks to be in his late thirties, immaculate in a tailored suit, silk tie, and waxed shoes. His hair is slicked back, balding at the center. Without a glance at the crowd of neighbors, he strides quickly toward Reza.

"You must be Reza!" the man says, throwing his arms wide for an embrace. Stunned, Reza stands like a statue before him.

The crowd murmurs: Who is this wealthy dandy with a fancy car and a chauffeur, and why would he come to the dilapidated Karbassi place? What would anybody want with that poor boy, Reza?

The man pulls Reza into his chest in a warm fatherly embrace. Reza has no idea who this man is. Then, after a few moments, the man pushes Reza back to stare into his eyes. "You have your father's eyes," he says tenderly. "God rest his soul." Then, noticing the crowd about them, he asks Reza, "Well, aren't you going to welcome your uncle?"

The man who steps into the courtyard is now known as Khan Amu Iranpour. Twenty-six years ago, it was he, Mehdy, and his older brother, Ahmad, whom Abolghassem banished for wearing the British uniforms of the South Persian Rifles. When the Shah decreed in 1927 that every man must have a family name, uncle Mehdy, whom Abolghassem barred from using the Karbassi name, claimed the name Iranpour, which means "full of Iran" or "love of Iran."

Mehdy had dedicated his name to his father's nationalist spirit. But Abolghassem offered no chance of reconciliation as long as Mehdy was connected to the British. Mehdy, like his brother Ahmad, never saw his father again.

Once inside the courtyard, Reza closes the gates behind his uncle and guides him to the formal room. Here Mahmoud once welcomed his guests to sit in the splendor of wall-to-wall layers of Karbassi rugs. Now the rugs are gone—sold to support Reza and his sisters. Reza gestures to the cushions on the carpetless stone floor. He helps his uncle down to the floor and then watches as he struggles to fold his legs in the traditional position. Has his uncle been sitting in British chairs for so long that he can no longer sit Persian style?

Soodabeh enters carrying tea, her rubber sandals snapping against her heels. Two beakers and a bowl of sugar rest on a silver tray that belonged to their mother, Soghra. The tray is hand-etched silver with intricate designs of flowers, birds, and vines with delicate leaves. It is the last bit of their parents' wealth that has not been bartered away, a mere whisper of a bygone era. The light amber glasses seem dull against the brilliance of the tray.

Soodabeh bends to offer tea to the elegantly dressed man. Her hands nervously rattle the tray. Everything in the room reminds her of their poverty. She turns quickly to leave.

Khan Amu Iranpour beckons her to sit, telling her he wants them to get to know each other. Soodabeh kneels next to Reza while Khan Amu looks pensively around the room. They remain quiet for quite some time.

Finally, Khan Amu speaks. "You know the story of the South Persian Rifles and my father's fury. I offer no explanation and no apology. The British saw something in me and they made me a second lieutenant, the lowest officer rank. But not long after that, my commanding officer asked if I might like to go to school—to get a formal education. I was sent to Isfehan to attend the Christian College that the British built there.

"Isfehan is an ancient Persian city, the magical city of culture and knowledge. I buried myself in books and studied. I burrowed into studying like a thirsty man in the desert. Soon I came to the attention of the college president himself, a man by the name of Bishop Thompson. He said I was an exceptional student and we became friends. When I finished at Christian College, he called me to his office. It was already arranged—I would go to study in Delhi, which I was assured was a much better education than the British could provide in Iran.

"It was my first trip out of Iran. I spent two years studying in India. Upon graduation, my friend Bishop Thompson paid my way to England for more graduate work."

Reza and Soodabeh listen to their uncle as if he's reading a storybook. They are mesmerized by the things he's done, the places he's seen. For Reza, imagining life outside of Kerman is entirely new. It is as if his uncle opened the front gates of the compound and invited the world in.

"When I got to England, I had my choice of jobs. I studied at night and worked by day. British companies operating in Iran needed Iranian nationals who could manage their interests. Among the companies was the Anglo-Persian Oil Company."

The Anglo-Persian Oil Company was formed in 1908 after the first discovery of oil in Southern Iran, near Abadan, the Masjet Soleiman field. After this discovery, the British led the exploration, refining, production, and export of the oil. Masjet Soleiman thus became British property.

"Abolghassem would rise from his grave to smite me with his staff. He would have said that it was treason to work for a foreign power with the rights to Iran's oil. But I took the job with the Anglo-Persian Oil Company."

Khan Amu Iranpour laces his fingers together and rests them in his lap. His brows furrow and his lips press together. He takes a sip of his tea, wetting his mouth. His words now come slowly, painfully. He seems to be dragging the words out of a deep cave.

"In London, I met an English girl, Elizabeth."

He circles his thumbs atop his interlaced fingers. He stares at the wall. His eyes fall on a tea leaf floating in his beaker.

"Her hair was golden and her eyes were blue. Delicate like crystal—clear crystal. Sweet and pleasant as saffron nectar."

He swirls his beaker watching the tea leaf float in circles.

"We got married soon after we met. My life became sweetness.

"Then Anglo-Persian decided to send me back to Iran, to Abadan, to supervise the refineries there. Elizabeth wanted to come with me. I told her Abadan sits on the edge of the Persian

Gulf. It is primitive. It is lonely. There is scorching heat. No place for a delicate crystal. She resisted. England would no longer be home if we were not together, she told me. Nothing could change her mind. Her own parents cried hysterically right by the side of the train, begging her to stay. Foolishly in love, she followed."

Khan Amu Iranpour pauses.

"Foolishly in love," he says after a while, his voice from a distant place and time. Then, as if awakened by reality, he continues. "For a while everything seemed rosy.

"We arrived in Abadan, and Elizabeth discovered she was pregnant. I had to work long hours and was often away on business for several days. I hired several servants to keep Elizabeth company. She stayed in the compound because all around us was nothing but dry, desolate land. She used to love the nights. When the desert air cooled, she'd laze and watch the star-filled skies. She'd say our stars—Iran's stars—were like grapes hanging from the vine, fooling you into believing you can pluck them. The desert was a world away from hers. Untouched. Still. Peaceful.

"Then one night in July, brutally hot, she was sprawled on a hammock rocking her large pregnant belly. Out of nowhere, a bearded man with a dagger jumped in front of her. Elizabeth's scream brought all the servants running. She passed out.

"Several days later I returned to find Elizabeth still cowering in the corner of our room. The servants told me how they had found her passed out on the ground. The assailant, whom they never found, had run into the darkness. He must have been frightened by the sight of a white woman—a ghost.

"She was never the same. She no longer watched the night sky. She did not dare peek at the stars or step out onto the veranda to be alone.

"Two months later, Elizabeth gave birth to our baby boy. We rejoiced. She smiled for the first time in months. I told her that our son is strong. Elizabeth prayed that he indeed would be strong, a desire so great that she decided to name our son Rostam."

"Rostam," he says again, with a sigh followed by silence.

"That valiant mythical hero," he reluctantly continues.

"Elizabeth chose that name as his shield. Did she think that she could not protect him? That I couldn't protect him? I don't know."

Unlacing his fingers, Khan Amu wipes several beads of sweat from his brow and then places his moist palms on his thighs. He loosens his tie and unclasps his shirt's top button. Reza and Soodabeh sit statue-like in front of him. Khan Amu continues.

"As Rostam grew, Elizabeth seemed more like herself. When Rostam turned six months old, our servant asked permission to take the day off to see an ailing relative in a village nearby. Elizabeth agreed. After the servant left, Elizabeth decided to give Rostam a bath. She rarely did that. It was the job of the servant. But on that particular day, Elizabeth, most likely hoping to cool Rostam, drew a bath of cool water.

"I can see it all in my head. She kneels by him, gently pouring water on Rostam's baby skin. Rostam giggles and kicks about." Khan Amu revels in the image of that moment. He doesn't want to move forward with his story. There's a long pause. Then, as if something shoves him forward, he continues in a barely perceptible voice.

"Elizabeth gets up to grab a bar of soap, or a towel. But she must have gotten up too quickly. She passed out. And, when she came to, she found Rostam face down in the water . . . dead.

"Her screams pierced the desert. She tore her hair out, clawed at her face until she drew blood, she wailed. We didn't know how to go from one minute to the next.

"From then on, she had to be sedated to keep her from doing harm to herself. But the drugs didn't help. She refused to speak. It wasn't safe to leave her alone. I took her to Isfehan to see British doctors. They said to send her back to England. They said that she blamed Iran for her anguish. I immediately arranged for Elizabeth to return to England on a private flight. She would be met by her parents. To keep her safe, I admitted her into a hospital for the night." Khan Amu seems to be speeding up to finish his story now; he wants to get it over with.

"The next day I rushed to the hospital so we could have a few hours together before her flight.

"My friend Bishop Thompson came with me. I ran to her room. There were several nurses by her door. I tried to go in, but a nurse stopped me. She had a note. It was from Elizabeth—I knew her writing. I knew she was gone. I fell to my knees.

"Bishop Thompson read the note aloud: 'Don't cry my Rostam. I am coming to you.'

"She had hung herself from a tree in the garden of the hospital."

By now night has begun to fall over them as they sit on the floor in the guest room. The color of the room has changed, from an afternoon orange to an evening gray. Soodabeh gets up and lights a kerosene lamp by the doorway. Its dim light warms the room and moths begin to dance around it. The three sit together in silence for a time, overcome and bereft, ravaged and chilled. Reza and Soodabeh stare blankly into their laps. Khan Amu Iranpour somberly rubs his finger where his wedding band used to be. The second hand of his gold watch clicks forward, its ticking sound loud enough for them all to hear.

Then, as if suddenly yanked from a spell, Khan Amu finds his way back from the memory that has engulfed him. Forcing a sad smile, he says, "I'm not here to burden your already heavy hearts. It's not the place where I want us to begin.

"You are the children of Mahmoud, my half-brother. I have a duty to you and my duty is to tell you to go on. You have no choice," he says, "but you do have help. It's time we put our past in the past and move on. That's why I am here." He slaps his hands on his thigh and looks up at the sad faces looking at him. Turning to Reza he says, "How would you like to have a job?"

Reza looks back at him blankly.

He repeats, "A job, Reza, a job!"

Two days later, the chauffer-driven car returns, once again drawing curious neighbors. This time Khan Amu Iranpour has come to deliver the letter from the NIOC that offers Reza a job. Khan Amu has personally signed it. It is dated December, 21, 1946. The eve of the winter solstice.

Tehran
1957

Once traditional and underdeveloped, the face of Tehran has changed dramatically. The transformation started in the 1920s, when Reza Khan hired German urban planners to design a modern city. However, Iran is a country of long traditions, and modernization was not universally accepted. His efforts were further thwarted by World War II.

In 1941, Anglo-Soviet forces, a coalition of British, Commonwealth, and Soviets troops, marched through Iran and forced Reza Khan to abdicate. They replaced him with his own son, Mohammad Reza. Even though Iran had proclaimed neutrality, the Anglo-Soviet alliance claimed that Iran was collaborating with Nazi Germany. They claimed that Iran's new name was a cognate of an Aryan word meaning "Land of Aryans," too close to Hitler's Aryan master race. Replacing Reza Khan with Muhammad Reza would give them the puppet ruler they needed in Iran to stabilize the region.

Mohammad Reza Shah Pahlavi gave himself three titles: His Imperial Majesty, King of Kings, Light of the Aryan and Bozorg Arteshtārān (Head of the Warriors). Everyone believed the Shah was invincible, but in 1951, Muhammad Mosaddegh was voted by the Iranian parliament to become prime minister. In effect, they ousted the Shah and voted Mosaddegh as their leader.

Mossadegh was known for his passionate aversion to foreign intervention. He demanded the nationalization of the Iranian oil industry. In a famous speech, he told his countrymen:

> *Our long years of negotiations with foreign countries . . .*
> *have yielded no results thus far. With the oil revenues,*
> *we could meet our entire budget and combat poverty,*
> *disease, and backwardness among our people . . . [With]*
> *the elimination of the power of the British company, we*
> *would also eliminate corruption and intrigue, by means*
> *of which the internal affairs of our country have been*

influenced. Once this tutelage has ceased, Iran will have achieved its economic and political independence.

Mossadegh reminded his people that the Anglo-Persian Oil Company was British property, that it was formed in the earlier part of the century when a large field was discovered in the southern region of Iran, an area known as Masjet Soleiman. Because it was British manpower that led the exploration, refining, production, and export of petroleum, the British had claimed it to be their property. Mossadegh wanted his country's oil back. And the populace supported him. In fact, he had the support of many people across the Middle East who saw him as an anti-imperialist.

In England, however, Winston Churchill not only saw Mossadegh's secular rule as a threat to England's control of Iran's oil, he also feared Iran was moving closer to their communist enemy, Russia. He warned Dwight Eisenhower, then U.S. president, of Iran's Soviet leanings.

Two years later, in 1953, at the request of British MI6, the American CIA organized a coup in Iran. Operation Ajax removed Mossadegh from power and restored Iran to the rule of Mohammad Reza Shah Pahlavi. Mossadegh was tried for treason and sentenced to three years in prison. Following his release, he was confined to house arrest for the remainder of his life.

With the Shah successfully restored to power, it was now the Americans, not the British, who had a vested interest in Iran. Still, Britain maintained inextricably tight links with the company it had established, the one now called the National Iranian Oil Company, known to all as NIOC.

* * *

On a sunny November morning in Tehran, Reza deftly follows his daily routine. He kisses five-year-old Keyhan on the cheek as the boy mimics driving a car with a pot lid. He tells Akhtar what he wants for dinner. She clears his breakfast plate, her stomach protruding with a seven-month pregnancy. Reza picks up his briefcase and heads downstairs to the metal-gated courtyard where he parks his petite Fiat. Before he pulls out of the courtyard, he checks the knot of his necktie in the rearview mirror and straightens the collar of the shirt Akhtar has starched and ironed. He then carefully backs up the car, leaving his rented house in a well-to-do middle-class neighborhood of northern Tehran. From this gentrified and developed quadrant, it takes Reza no more than half an hour to get to his office. He drives along the city's spacious, cleanly paved boulevards that are lined with trees wearing vast leaf crowns.

Reza passes the NIOC sign, the name inscribed on copper and framed by a huge slab of black marble, on his daily route to work. Stepping into his brightly lit office, Reza feels as proud as he does every day. When Khan Amu Iranpour hired his nephew, he had no idea what a dedicated and committed employee he was bringing on board. He had no idea that his nephew would be completely engrossed in the job. The job became Reza's identity. Consequently, Reza has risen speedily through company ranks. After only two years of overseeing a refueling depot station, the job that Khan Amu Iranpour arranged for him, Reza was promoted to a job in Tehran. Something about the enthusiasm and vigor with which he commanded his platoon of sunburned human mules on that parched stretch of desert land outside of Kerman, the way he managed the illiterate workers hauling fuel for planes that were making a pit stop between Dehli and Tehran, gained the attention of Charles Edgart. Son of a wealthy textile factory owner and an English mother, Edgart had friends within the Shah's inner circle. He and Reza met when Edgart was flying to Dehli. During stops in Kerman, Edgart befriended Reza. It did not take long before he promoted Reza to the Tehran office.

Now, after eleven years, Reza still maintains the same zest with which he showed up to work on his very first day.

So this morning, when he snaps open his briefcase and his secretary walks in with his customary beaker of tea, Reza is already a proud NIOC employee. But as she places beside his tea a letter sealed with a crown, Reza is struck with disbelief. He opens the five-sentence letter holding the company orders and reads it several times. Adrenaline pumps through his veins and the words on the page swim as he tried to gather his thoughts. Crossing his arms and reclining back in his chair, Reza looks out through his office window.

The sixteen floors of the NIOC building make it the tallest in Tehran. Sitting behind his desk, Reza can see the majestic mountain range of Alborz on the city's northern horizon over the rooftops of neighboring buildings. The jagged, snow-capped mountains provide a dramatic backdrop to this blossoming city. Thinking about the letter lying on his desk, Reza's eyes—as if pulled by a rope—turn toward the mountain's tallest peak: Damavand. The place where Rostam, a hero of Persia, performed his legendary feats. Reza looks at Damavand, an immortalized site of triumph, feeling that it is, like the recently opened letter, symbolic of his ascent through the company ranks.

The mountain also reminds Reza of his weekly predawn hike with his colleagues. Smiling, he thinks about breaking the news to them. How appropriate to share his upcoming assignment with them as they climb up the mountain, the rocky ground crunching beneath their feet.

On Fridays, the day of the week when businesses are closed and Tehran's usual bustle quiets to an eerie hush, Damavand becomes a popular recreational destination for city dwellers like Reza and his colleagues. Stars still shine brightly overhead when they assemble at its foot. Wearing casual clothing, a stark contrast to their office garb of heavily starched shirts and ties, Reza and his friends share stories from the office, tell jokes, or plan family vacations to the Caspian Sea, where they stay in NIOC-owned villas. Along the way they pass vendors who sell dates, fresh walnuts, eggs—all types of goods, lined up on their weathered canvas cloths and illuminated by kerosene lamps. They often see an ambitious vendor squatting characteristically by a log fire and churning a pot of *abgoosht,* meat soup. He offers the early morning hikers a steaming bowl. Reza usually passes them with little notice. He prefers to eat at a restaurant at the summit. There he likes to sit back on a large wooden bench covered with tribal carpets and have waiters rotate platters of food before him. Yogurt, dates, eggs, and hearth-cooked bread— all of it carried up the mountain on the backs of mules.

Indeed, Reza thinks to himself now, still staring at the faraway mountains, his colleagues will be surprised to hear the news. Imaging the look on each of their faces, he says to himself, "Who would have thought?" He marvels at the word "London!" To Reza the name flows so mellifluously that it seems to ring with music. In this day and age, when social and financial mobility in Tehran have become contingent on how closely one follows the standards of Western countries, every aspiring bureaucrat like Reza hopes for the opportunity to spend time abroad. It will earn him the title of *doreh dideh,* which carries a status all its own. Out of the thousands of employees on the company roster he can hardly believe they have picked him for the overseers training post in London. So dearly is it coveted within the company that it carries near-mystical qualities. Only the most valued employees get such a chance. Studying in London will quicken his already accelerated rise through the company ranks. Reza looks out his window at Damavand and thinks, I'll hike right to the summit.

Outside his office door, in a long corridor, Reza hears the steps of a passerby echoing loudly on the polished marble floors. Taking a deep breath, Reza shifts his gaze from the mountain view to a twelve-inch flag resting at the head of his uncluttered, polished black desk. Made of velvet and edged by a draping of golden silk yarn, the flag stands erect and patriotic. A similar flag rests atop the desk of every employee in the building, an element of company conformity. Just like the large black-and-white portrait of Iran's current monarch, Mohammad Reza Pahlavi, that hangs on every office wall. Throughout the course of an average day, it's not uncommon for the photograph to capture Reza's attention. The Shah's pose, with his right hand raised in the air, incites simultaneous feelings of pride and obedience. Is that raised hand the gesture of a champion inspiring his subjects? Or is it a sign of his dictatorial omnipotence?

Several months earlier, Dr. Eghbal, the country's prime minister, issued a directive setting exact standards for the flag, specifying how the Pahlavi crest should be displayed at all times. Then he mandated its delivery, along with a letter, to all government personnel. The letter embodies the Pahlavi government's effort to instill a visceral sense of commitment to a modern Iran. It states that "Iran is a proud nation . . . intent on progress . . . steadfast towards modernity." This is an ethos that Reza wholeheartedly adheres to. For him, being a proud employee is tantamount to patriotism. In today's Iran, that means loyalty to the Pahlavi monarchy.

Reza stares at the flag for quite some time, mesmerized. His ego is pumped. He picks the flag up from its base and waves it back and forth. Reza regards the smoothness of the fabric as the three horizontal bands, green above white above red, dance with the movement of his wrist. Inside the folds of the lightweight fabric is a medallion that distinguishes this particular flag from that of any other period. A lion stands boldly in the center of the three-color flag, holding a sword. Rays of sunshine form a fan above the beast.

Around the lion, two olive branches cross and join, cradling the Pahlavi crown, the symbol of the regime that Reza feels has opened up the world to him.

Reza waves the flag once more. It briefly flutters, then rests, draping the Pahlavi crest within its folds. Sliding the flag back into its base, Reza picks up the intercom and buzzes his secretary, Ashraf Khanom—a woman of about twenty-five who wears miniskirts and an abundance of makeup—to bring tea. He usually revels in watching her parade in and out of his office. But not today. Taking his index finger off the intercom box, consumed with personal satisfaction, Reza breathes in, cups his hands behind his head, and smiles a self-congratulatory smile. If all goes well, he calculates, he should be in London by the spring of '58, just short of five months away.

On the snowy seventh day of January, 1958, two months shy of Reza's assignment to London, Akhtar gives birth to their second son, Kambiz. He is a striking infant with flawless olive skin, round cherry eyes, and plump lips. But he is fretful. Cranky and ill-tempered. He screams and squirms until he lies in his mother's arms. Nothing soothes him other than Akhtar's bosom. Akhtar strokes her newborn's head gently and wonders whether his attachment to her is so strong that it causes him pain.

Narragansett
2005

The noise of the lawnmower from across the street has quieted down. The late-morning chatter of birds and the racket of the cicadas and crickets now pipe into the garage. Akhtar stands fixed in her spot, the small photograph of 18-month-old Kambiz in hand.

The dumpster that Kambiz has sent over for their move waits in the driveway to swallow its next load. The garbage bin is tipped over at her feet. She is surrounded by boxes—like a frozen courtroom audience looking imploringly at the judge.

Akhtar stares into her son's eyes in the photograph. He seems to accuse her. A defendant before a judge, a mother before her son. She has to explain things to him.

"I had no choice," she pleads to the jury of cardboard boxes. "In Iran, a wife must follow her husband. I didn't have a choice."

Are her words a confession, apology, or excuse, she wonders. The photograph is a rebuke, and she knows it. But we must endure, she thinks, and that time in London was the longest, the hardest for a mother to live through.

Her regret lingers and probes. It continues to condemn. So she tells the photograph, "I wish you'd only known, Kambiz *joon*. Let me tell you about that period of our lives." She wishes Kambiz himself were present to hear this story now. If only he had the time, they could pull up two plastic folding chairs from the corner of the garage, and she'd tell him her story. If he only took the time . . .

She'd say, "Reza left for London in the spring to look for a place to live and to begin his studies at Tuttingham College. Meanwhile, I went to live with my parents in Kerman. Once he found a flat and got settled, he sent us a letter.

"It was September when Reza's letter arrived. 'Bring Keyhan. He can learn English in the school. But leave Kambiz with your parents. There's no room and his wailing will disturb the landlady upstairs."

"Leave Kambiz." Akhtar remembers. The words still stun her, a kick in her gut.

"Leave Kambiz." The words spilled out on the page like a bloodstain.

How could she leave her baby—only nine months old and still nursing?

Kerman
1959

After a year, little Kambiz no longer cries for his mother at night. He nestles next to his grandmother, Tayebeh, playing with her simple carnelian ring. He falls asleep holding her finger. By day he plays in the courtyard where Akhtar had played. He toddles into the kitchen to find Tayebeh, just as Akhtar had followed the smells of fresh bread to find Jan-Bibi.

He prowls around the courtyard. One day they find Kambiz by the side of the courtyard sitting inside a bucket of dates, covered head to toe in the sugary fruit, chewing away. He seems happy now.

There is a new photography studio in Kerman. About a week after he plucked Kambiz from the bucket of dates, Sadegh carries Kambiz in his arms past the dome-shaped mud house to the center of town. In the large empty room, he props Kambiz up on a stool while the photographer stands beside his camera and a large lamp. Together, Sadegh and the photographer work to get the little boy to smile. Nothing works. The light grows hotter. Then Sadegh fishes into the pocket of his sagging peasant coat.

A date from the pocket—a smile from Kambiz.

When the photograph is ready, Sadegh slips it into his coat and heads straight to the post and telegraph office. The post office is a crisp, modern building, which, in contrast to Kerman's slow, unfrenzied pace, swarms with people.

For a while, Sadegh stands lost in the rush of people and the blur of voices in front of the brick post office. He wants to send Kambiz's photograph to Akhtar, but he has no way of writing his daughter's address in England. It must be written in Roman letters. He can barely scratch out Farsi.

He paces back and forth, inside and out, asking for help. Finally, Sadegh is directed to a man who writes on behalf of unlettered people.

"Agha," Sadegh bows to the man. "I am here to ask your kindness to write a letter for me."

"Two *gheroon*."

"Agha, this should be a favor for an old man."

"*Boroh baba*—go away." The man turns to help someone else.

Sadegh stands staring at the man. He once had watched Akhtar producing the magic of writing, those swift, sailing lines of Farsi. Now he watches the man's deft strokes, and then his pudgy fingers pocketing the coins.

Sadegh bows to the man again. The man looks away and takes another customer.

Sadegh refuses to move. He keeps his eyes on the man. After a few more customers, the man leans back against the brick wall of the post office. He reaches into a bowl of pistachios and pops a few into his mouth.

In a soft voice, Sadegh tries again. "Agha, my daughter is far away—in England—and her baby . . ."

Sadegh shows the man the photograph of Kambiz. "She hasn't seen him for a year."

The man rolls a pistachio between his fingers. "One gheroon."

"Agha, please. In the name of Allah."

"I have to buy my paper, my pens . . ."

Sadegh holds out his envelope and the crumpled paper with the address on it. The man looks quickly around and then scribbles the address on the envelope in Roman letters.

Sadegh bows deeply and walks away. He has no letter to go along with the photograph, but he isn't sure what words to say anyway: That Kambiz is well? That he no longer cries? That her son loves dates? There should be more. He wants to tell her that he and Tayebeh are well. That the neighborhood bread lady still comes, and the smell of fresh bread still floats through the courtyard.

Sadegh also wants to tell Akhtar that her grandmother, Jan-Bibi, passed away. Knowing how close the two were, Sadegh would want to break the news gently. If he could write the words. He would reassure Akhtar that she passed away painlessly. How a fortnight earlier at the dinner *sofreh*, Tayebeh was passing her a slice of honeydew when they noticed that Jan-Bibi had fallen asleep. Silently, she left this world for the next. Even in passing, Sadegh wants to tell Akhtar, his mother had not wanted to burden anyone.

Sadegh wants to tell Akhtar so many things. He has the thoughts but cannot find the words. At least the photograph will tell her the most important thing.

Sadegh sends the letter by ground mail. Months later, when the envelope reaches Akhtar in London, she can't hold back her tears, even in front of the mailman who handed it to her.

London
1959

Akhtar rises early to fix breakfast for Reza. He eats quickly and rushes off to Tuttingham College. Keyhan eats his breakfast, and Akhtar cleans up in the tiny basement flat. She glances up at the one narrow window. The sliver of morning light is as grey as the English sky.

Keyhan is dressed like a proper English schoolboy: blue blazer, gray knickers, and a maroon-and-gold striped tie. After cleaning up the breakfast plates, Akhtar walks Keyhan to school.

She watches the other mothers with their children, some pushing prams with babies. It makes her heart ache with longing for her baby.

Keyhan runs ahead, shouting brightly to his friends.

"Moman, don't come with me, I can go myself!" he tells her.

In a flash, he blends in with all the uniformed boys laughing and jumping about. Akhtar stands watching him until he disappears inside the school. Then she walks home alone. Back in the flat, she puts the pillow to her chest and sobs in her loneliness. As she has done every day for three years.

Those years in London seemed longer than an eternity. For Akhtar, the basement flat is a prison cell. The return to Iran cannot come soon enough.

Then comes the day when they can return home. Three years she has waited. Three long years. It is 1961. Reza has spent all his savings on a Vauxhall Victor, a General Motors car, manufactured in England. He ordered it directly from the factory so that it could have a left-side steering wheel.

"We are going to drive this car back home to Iran," he tells Akhtar as if they are going home on a magic carpet.

To 10-year-old Keyhan, the Vauxhall Victor is also pure excitement. For both of them it is a toy come to life.

The Vauxhall is clean and shiny, with an elegant curved windscreen. The windscreen pillars slope backwards, like the Chevy Bel Air, made in America. The Vauxhall has a three-speed gear box, with the shift mounted on the steering column. And it uses the new grade of fuel, premium petrol.

They cross the English Channel by ferry and then take to the open roads of Europe. Akhtar sits alone in the back seat, while Keyhan takes over as navigator, serving as his father's co-pilot. Reza has taught him the ins and outs of the knobs and gauges. Reza gives Keyhan the map and trusts him to point out the roads they need to take. After three years in England, Keyhan speaks nearly perfect English. So along the way, whenever they need directions, Keyhan does the talking for his parents.

Keyhan loves the car, a love he shares with his father. Father and son are allies, friends on a mission. Reza dotes on Keyhan as if he were his only son. And Keyhan beams at his father. He feels indulged. He even takes hold of the steering wheel on the straight country roads.

Akhtar watches from the back seat. It seems that the winds of the roads are sweeping through the curved windshield, softening Reza. Did he ever feel the pain of not having Kambiz with them? She will never know.

On that long road, she struggles to keep her mind blank, feeling selfish for wanting to be home right away. While Reza and Keyhan fiddle with the gadgets on the dashboard, Akhtar daydreams of holding Kambiz. She imagines the touch of his skin, the warmth of his little body, his baby smell. His photograph is snug in her handbag, which rests in her lap. She yearns to hear Kembiz say, "Moman."

Reza feels like the conquering hero as they drive through Holland and France and on to Yugoslavia. He keeps calling out the sights—"The rolling green hills of Europe."

He is a conqueror, Akhtar thinks. He has earned the training in England and he is now coming home a knight, ready to climb the ranks of the National Iranian Oil Company. He is riding on premium grade petrol.

But for Akhtar it is all just one long road home.

When they reach the first Communist bloc country, they load the Vauxhall onto a freight train and board a passenger train to Tehran. The entire trip takes nearly a month.

Shortly after the train reaches Tehran, Sadegh and Tayebeh make the two-day bus trip from Kerman with three-year-old Kambiz.

Akhtar's heart feels like it is bursting through her chest as they wait in the hectic Tehran bus station. She searches the crowd for the little face she has pasted in her mind from her one photograph. The crowd streams by her like the blur of a sandstorm. The final seconds of separation are the hardest to bear. Then, like a miracle, like a shining beacon of light, Akhtar sees Sadegh and Tayebeh coming toward her. Kambiz appears like a brilliant prism of color walking between them.

Narragansett
2005

"I remember I ran toward you, reaching my arms out as far as they'd extend. I thought that once I held you then I could bury those three years away.

"When Sadegh brought you closer to me and gently told you, *een momanat hast,* this is your mother, you shied away. You ran and hid behind Tayebeh's chador and started to cry.

"I wanted to grab you, shake you, tell you that I AM your mother. I wanted to shout, to cry! I felt betrayed. I had suffered so much to reach that moment, only for you to reject me. I felt I had been slammed against a brick wall. I thought it was a nightmare. My own son not recognizing his mother. Ahh, that still pains me.

"'Don't worry,' they said. 'He's just shy, in a few days it will be like you never left,' they kept saying.

"But I remember now. Months passed. You didn't warm up to me, Kambiz. You squirmed and fidgeted if I tried to pick you up. I reluctantly came to accept the distance you needed from me. I was happy just to have you by my side again, under the same roof."

Akhtar looks around her. The boxes sit, still waiting for her attention, the jury patiently awaiting a verdict. The little photograph still seems to accuse her. There is silence between her and the tiny photograph she holds her in hand. She doesn't know what else to say.

Finally, she whispers, "*B'bakhsh,* forgive me."

She repeats, "*B'bakhsh,* Kambiz *joon,*" still needing to cleanse herself of her guilt.

Slowly she slides the photograph under a plastic pocket in a photo album, right next to his brother Keyhan's picture, in which he is wearing his British school uniform and flashing his 10-year-old smile. Then she turns around to pick up the trash beneath her feet.

Tehran
1961

The Tehran that Reza and Akhtar left behind is no longer the same. To them it is a new city. The oil boom has revved the engines of modernization. Everyone is after a pot of gold, looking for the slightest competitive edge and fervently cheering the supposed architect of this new wealth—the Shah.

Reza Shah Pahlavi's modernization efforts are being advertised as his White Revolution. He has extended worker participation in factories through a shares system. His Imperial Armed Forces have created an "Army of Knowledge" that travels to remote villages to foster literacy. And he has created a program to provide schoolchildren with nourishing food. He has instituted exams for theologians who want to become established clerics, making it difficult for any one individual to promote himself as a religious authority. And in a significant move that faced heavy opposition from the Islamic clergy, he has extended suffrage to women.

Nowadays, women in Tehran dress much like their counterparts in Europe. Beehives are the latest hair fashion. Heavy eye shadow, bright glossy lipstick, and miniskirts are also "in." Those who don the veil are seen as traditional; those who don't, modern.

With his new British credentials, Reza has been promoted. He spends long hours at the office, followed by business socializing. His British experience has given him social cachet and he is swept up by the social life of the bureaucratic community. At parties, he and his NIOC colleagues chat over glasses of scotch and whiskey, behaving like British and American businessmen.

In a separate room, the wives, too, mimic farangi, Western culture. Akhtar listens to conversations about fashion and jewelry and to the endless complaints about ignorant, lower class kolfats, the servants who never clean or cook properly. She hears the biting competitiveness about vacations and redecoration plans, and of children displaying signs of irrefutable genius.

The bustle of their life in Tehran soon draws a curtain on her memories of her three years of torment. Life moves on.

* * *

A woman flips the pages of Zan-e Rooz—*Today's Woman*—a new magazine being sold at kiosks around Tehran. The woman's eyelids, up to her brow, are painted a glossy pistachio green, her hair is elaborately teased and sculpted into a large bouffant rise atop her head, her lipstick is bright red, and her skirt, when she is seated, rides above her knees. She looks no different from the women Akhtar used to see in London, except that her skin is olive, not pale white. For a brief moment, the Mod appearance of this woman sharing the waiting room allows Akhtar's mind to wander. As the fashionable woman bats her thick false eyelashes in rhythm with the magazine pages she is slowly turning, Akhtar thinks how the anti-veiling edict, only twenty-five years in existence, has transformed the appearance of Iranian women.

Two seats away, to Akhtar's right, is another woman, sitting upright on a metal chair. From where she sits, Akhtar guesses the woman is roughly the same age, about thirty. Her head is bowed so low that it's hard to see her face. She didn't even lift her head when Akhtar walked in. Her eyes are cast down, appearing either deep in thought or deep in shame.

Sitting three seats away from Akhtar is yet another woman, this one draped in gold jewelry. Akhtar watched her check in. After she signed the slip the receptionist gave her, she took her seat, crossed one leg over the other, and began to impatiently pump her feet up and down, her stylish shoes swinging back and forth. Her gold dress must be from one of the posh boutiques on Takht-e Jamshid, the upscale shopping area in the western part of Tehran. The shopping center is named after the former capital of the Persian Empire, where majestic columns towered toward the sky and royal stairways spanned across the columns. Winged bulls with human heads were etched in limestone alongside a phoenix rising from the flames. Takht-e Jamshid shopping center has risen from the ashes to give Tehrooni women golden dresses, tight red skirts, and pistachio green eyeliner.

On the wall facing her, Akhtar sees a framed picture of a nurse in a white cap staring back. Her index finger is across her lips, motioning quiet. Not a sound—other than the flipping of magazine pages—can be heard in the room.

Akhtar wrings her hands nervously, taking her eyes off the stylish woman's shoes. Suddenly Akhtar gasps. There is an empty spot around her wrist. Missing is the watch that Sadegh gave her for finishing her sixth year of school. The simple one with the brown band and the bland clear face. It's been years since she's worn it. She put it away some time ago and now cannot recall where she placed it. Rubbing her wrist, Akhtar wonders why she misses it now.

Akhtar called for an appointment this morning and got in right away. Dr. Jandaghi is a distant relative and is not her usual doctor. For this appointment, she believed family would be better. Now she regrets it.

The past two weeks run through her mind. At first she had thought there must be some mistake. She considered her symptoms and rationalized that it must be the stomach bug that everyone at the dinner party had been talking about a few nights ago. Mrs. Farzan, whose husband works with Reza, said she looked pale and that it may not be the stomach bug. She said it was Tehran's water. Reza and Akhtar have been away for so long that it must be T.T., Tehran Tummy, Mrs. Farzan said, almost chuckling. It's what the Americans are calling it. There had been a trickle of laughter from the rest of the NIOC wives in their host's the brightly lit parlor with the elaborate chandelier. Akhtar had felt relieved. But the more she thought about it, as the guests chatted away, the more it seemed clear to her that a stomach bug wouldn't have lasted for as long as this. Then, yesterday morning, she had run into the bathroom retching. She instantly knew that this was neither a stomach flu nor T.T.

She and Reza talked about it briefly before he left for the office. He thought the timing was all wrong. "Can't you see how busy I am," he asked? "Besides, I still need to save money for buying a house." Then he told her to make an appointment with Dr. Jandaghi. "The sooner the better," he added as he walked out the door.

Akhtar didn't want to go to a doctor. Certainly not for this. She tried to solve the problem herself: sitting in a tub of scalding-hot water, jumping rope, and reaching her hands above her head. She thought one of those might do the trick. She tried everything. She even punched her abdomen hoping to rid it from her body. Nothing happened.

This morning, Reza's sister Soodabeh came to the house to be with the kids so Akhtar could go to her appointment. Akhtar was too embarrassed to tell her sister-in-law the reason for the doctor's visit. She feels Soodabeh has enough on her mind these days. Her husband is a difficult man. He is twenty-five years older and is a respected general in the Shah's military. But he is as stern at home as he is at work. Everyone addresses him as *Timsar*, General. Even Soodabeh.

It was Reza who had decided that Timsar would make a good husband for his youngest sister. Soodabeh had been living with Reza and Akhtar for years. When Reza received his London assignment, he needed to find a home for his sister. He married both his sisters to men old enough to be their father. Timsar wears round, wire-rimmed glasses and nearly always has on his military uniform. He's a chain smoker and has a heavy hand when it comes to disciplining Soodabeh. Soodabeh often confides in Akhtar about her husband, but asks that Akhtar keep it between the two of them, lest Reza get upset. Akhtar believes everything Soodabeh tells her, but she herself has only seen Timsar's kinder side—for example, his penchant to donate what he can to orphanages. He seems to have a weak spot for homeless kids.

At this point, Timsar and Soodabeh only have two kids, both about the same age as Kambiz. Glancing down at her hands, Akhtar wonders what Soodabeh and the kids are doing now, glad that the cousins are together. It'll be good for Kambiz, she thinks. Akhtar senses that Kambiz may finally be climbing out of his shell, that he seems to be inching his way toward her. This morning, with his thumb in his mouth, he had clambered onto her lap. They had nearly cuddled into a hug when the doorbell rang. It was Soodabeh. Soon after that she left for her appointment, not realizing she had lost an opportunity to stitch Kambiz back to herself—one among the many that seem to pass by. Her days are consumed with housework, the nights filled with parties. Maybe her mother, Tayebeh, is right, Akhtar reassures herself as she sits in the hushed waiting room. Maybe all he needs is time.

Akhtar looks about the windowless room and sighs with longing. A dull ache washes over her. She wants it to end and damns herself for wanting it so. She looks at the clock on the wall. The small hand is on eleven, the bigger one inching toward eight. She feels a tremendous desire to get up and leave. But, she's afraid of Reza's reaction. If he finds out she didn't go through with the procedure, he'll surely be furious. There's no way out of this.

For the past hour, Akhtar has tried hard to steer her mind from the appointment at hand. But as much as she tries, she is no longer capable of holding back the thought that keeps coming to her. Alas, letting her guard down, her thoughts escape from the waiting room. In a far corner of her mind, she enters a solitary place where she and a newborn baby cuddle—like a dream she used to have in London. But this one is so palpable that she nearly reaches to touch the newborn's fresh, delicate skin. Putting her head close to smell its deliciously sweet scent, she can almost hear the soft wheezing of its breath, its heart pulsating with life. Then, as if the baby is magically transformed, Akhtar sees a little bouncing girl before her, skipping rope, gregarious and carefree. Her deep, black eyes shine with laughter. The little girl stops to look at Akhtar, curiously, but in a condemning sort of way. Her look is piercing, burning through to her heart. And then, as if again transformed, she envisions a young woman sitting next to her, holding her hands. Akhtar is no longer young: protruding blue veins contour her wrinkled brown skin, foretelling some future moment. A light breeze coming through a half-open window caresses her skin. A translucent cotton drape wafts back and forth. The young woman drapes one arm over Akhtar's shoulder while Akhtar leans in to rest her weary head on the young woman's chest, feeling that all she wants out of life is to be buried in the folds of that embrace.

A white-uniformed nurse with a cap has appeared in the waiting room. "Mrs. Karbassi," she calls out authoritatively, startling Akhtar from her reverie. Akhtar does not respond. In the space of a silent breath or two, the nurse calls out again, "Mrs. Karbassi?"

As Akhtar slowly rises from the metal chair, she briefly catches the eye of the woman who has been staring at her lap the entire time. It's the first time their eyes meet. Her dark brown eyes, Akhtar thinks, seem sad. It's as though she's watching a lamb go to slaughter. Feeling disgraced, Akhtar thinks to herself that she *is* going toward a slaughter . . . but not her own.

When Akhtar approaches, the nurse tells her, "Dr. Jandaghi will see you now. But if it's okay, he'd like to have a word with you first."

Akhtar follows the nurse down a seemingly endless hallway, her head drooping and shoulders hunched. Guilt weighs on her more than she could ever have imagined.

After her appointment, Akhtar takes a bus home, a red double-decker like the kind she used to take in London. She climbs the winding stairwell and takes a seat on the upper level. She plops down heavily, a drop that's weighted by both fatigue and shame. She feels mentally troubled and physically nauseated. She feels drained.

Deep inside, mixed with her anxiety, is relief.

She pulls herself across the narrow rectangular seat, closer to the window. As she settles in, the hot black vinyl seat stings her legs. From this spot, Akhtar is able to see the street below. Sunrays beat down on her ferociously. She squints, but relishes the warmth it affords her at this particular moment, when the chill of the doctor's office clings to her bones. She leans her head close to the window. Her reflection stares back: a 29-year-old woman who has just experienced one of her toughest decisions. She had never envisioned how difficult it would be to confront this dilemma. When Reza told her to make an appointment with Dr. Jandaghi, she hadn't imagined that the decision would cause her such emotional turmoil. It really hadn't hit her until she stepped into the doctor's office. Then the gravity of it dawned on her and self-disdain started to flow through her like boiling water. Now, meeting her own eyes in the reflection of the bus window, a voice within asks, "How can you justify this to yourself?"

The red bus maneuvers its way through the Tehran traffic. Akhtar's body sways side to side. The rocking comforts her. She continues to regard her reflected image. This time, something more superficial catches her attention—splotches of black mascara under her eyes that reveal her gloom. She snaps her purse open and takes out a handkerchief, still damp with the torrent of tears that she shed in Dr. Jandaghi's office. She wipes each eye and sniffles. The appointment with Dr. Jandaghi had taken no more than an hour. Her eyes fill with tears again as she thinks back to it. She realizes that she'll never forget what happened this morning, that it will undoubtedly leave an everlasting impression. Her hand involuntarily moves toward her abdomen. She feels strangely glad that she has paid a visit to Dr. Jandaghi.

Dr. Jandaghi had convinced her to postpone her decision for another week. His suggestion had immediately lifted a huge burden off Akhtar's back. Her relief was so great that it was palpable—she'd felt able to breathe again. Yet, just as quickly as that dread had been relieved, it was replaced with another. She knew Reza would not be pleased to hear about the delay. He wants to be rid of this quickly. Telling him of the postponement will be difficult; telling him she wants to abandon the idea will be impossible. How will she persuade him? she asks herself, digging her nails into her palms.

While she tries to figure out how to broach the topic with Reza, she notices something outside her window. Standing at a traffic light are a mother and daughter, their hands locked, waiting to cross the street. There's nothing extraordinary about them, nothing striking. But at this moment they capture Akhtar's attention. "I want this baby," she dares to tell herself. Nothing has ever been more certain as this feeling she has now. She knows she now has enough assurance to challenge her husband, however difficult it might be. Akhtar then notices that amid the shuffle of pedestrians, the little girl skips alongside her mother to the other side of the road. Gently patting her belly, Akhtar tells herself, "This, I feel, is a girl."

That evening, Reza arrives home late from work. Kambiz and Keyhan are already in bed when Akhtar hears the Vauxhaull's engine pull up in front of their apartment. Every muscle in her body stiffens at the sound. She hustles to serve Reza his dinner. She ladles his favorite dish—buttery rice with lentils and dates—onto a plate and sets it on the kitchen table. At its side, she places a glass of carbonated yogurt drink, a spoon and fork, right and left, respectively. Then, gulping down a lump in her throat, she waits for Reza to make his way up the stairs and into their second-floor apartment.

He walks in, places his briefcase by the entryway, loosens his tie, and walks straight to the table.

"*Salaam,*" Akhtar says tentatively, while Reza pulls his chair in toward the table.

"*Salaam.*" He responds casually, as if he's forgotten that this was the day of her appointment. For a brief moment, Akhtar wonders if she can avoid this talk. She thinks that maybe it is better not to remind him. Then, her better senses convince her the conversation is inevitable. She seats herself across the table. Once her husband has had several spoonfuls, she begins . . . cautiously.

"Doctor Jandaghi asked if I could change my appointment to next week," she says, breaking the silence between them.

"*Chera?* Why?" Reza asks curtly, stuffing his mouth with rice.

"He thought . . ." She starts meekly, but then summons greater courage. Determinedly, she says, "We should think about it for another week."

Keeping his frustration in check, Reza takes a drink and asks, "Why do we need to talk about it?"

Akhtar bites her lip. She already feels her heart racing. Her mouth is dry, as it always is when she's nervous. She decides it's better not to answer just yet.

Reza blurts, "He's not the one who'll have to pay for its bills!" His voice swells. He holds his spoon like a pitchfork. "Well, will he?" he asks, glaring at Akhtar, whose eyes refuse to meet his.

She does not respond. A few minutes pass. There's nothing to say. Reza, though clearly agitated, continues to eat. Then, after what seems a long time, Akhtar decides to press on. Softly, she tells her husband, "Doctor Jandaghi wants to make sure that we've thought about it . . . that we won't end up regretting this decision." Her voice is almost a whisper. She doesn't want the boys to wake up to find their father angry—again.

But Reza, his face red with exasperation, says, "I've already told you that two boys are enough! That's all the children we need. I can't support another one." Now shouting, he repeats, "I just can't!"

The echo of his loud voice lingers between them for quite some time. From across the table, Akhtar looks at her husband's tightened face. His eyes are now cast down on the table, refusing to meet hers.

"Karbassi," she begins, "I know you have the burden of responsibility to provide for us. You're the breadwinner. You've carried this burden since youth, long before you started your own family. This responsibility . . . is yours. I understand that. You have the right to consider how we'll manage with another child.

But this one . . ." she rests her hand on her stomach, "is like Kambiz and Keyhan. Like your brother Javad, God rest his soul. How can we dispose of this life?" She stops and notes her husband's silence.

She continues, suddenly assertive. "I've followed you from Kerman to Tehran. Then, again, I followed you to England, and I left Kambiz behind like you asked me to. I'm a follower. But on this . . . I mean . . . for this . . ." she says, and drops her eyes to her belly, "I will not follow you." She ends her sentence with conviction she didn't know she possessed.

Except for the ticking of the kitchen clock and the drip of the faucet, the two sit in silence for quite some time. Something in Akhtar's words, or maybe in her tone, gives Reza pause. Akhtar waits patiently. She knows there is nothing else she can say. Finally Reza takes a deep breath—the kind one takes before embarking on a new road. A breath that says he will hope for the best.

Akhtar understands his tacit response. "Merci," she says softly.

Narragansett
2005

"Khanom! telephone!" Reza calls to Akhtar from the living room.

Akhtar dashes through the vestibule to pick up the receiver in the kitchen. She already knows it's her daughter. She's always been able to sense it.

"*Allo?*" She says into the mouthpiece of the white receiver, which—connected to a badly twisted telephone wire— rests on a wall-mounted base, right next to a framed embroidery project that her daughter made when she was a young girl. As with the ceramic bowl her daughter made in the fourth grade, Akhtar has treasured this frame for years.

Sliding down on one of the chairs by the oval kitchen table, tightly gripping the receiver, she faces her daughter's framed sewing project.

"*Khoobi azizam,* Are you well my dear?" she asks her, looking at the embroidery of flowers, its tiny stitches and myriad colors drooping from an old-fashioned milk bottle.

Her daughter had stitched the milk bottle during their first summer in New York. During school vacation that year, Kambiz and Keyhan were old enough to go outside on their own. Her daughter remained restricted. New York City was far too bewildering for a nine-year-old, Akhtar had gauged. So whenever her daughter begged to go down to the building's playground, Akhtar tried to distract her with handicrafts and dangling art objects, like a hypnotic amulet, to keep her daughter inside. The milk bottle sewing kit she'd purchased from the drugstore was precisely that—amusement for her daughter, assurance for Akhtar.

Hanging beside the telephone, it serves as reminder of that first summer in America, of their awkward adjustment period, of Akhtar's fears. Especially the fear of losing her daughter. The fear that has been with her since that morning in the waiting room long, long ago.

"I was in the garage. *Areh,* there's still so much more to do . . . your father's not much help, all day in his chair. Today he's only managed to go through a box of his files."

They are physical replicas of one another, with their thick wavy hair, slender figures, and dark eyes—only the damages of age demarcate mother from daughter.

Lately, Akhtar has taken to comparing her life to her daughter's and Tayebeh's. She thinks of her daughter's fast-paced life. Always running around. Busy, busy. Work and books, work and books. Yet her own is so empty. Then she thinks about her mother, Tayebeh. How Tayebeh's world was defined by a community that knew her from birth. When she bought a satchel of saffron from a vendor in the bazaar, he'd ask after each family member by name. When she called on their tailor to sew their annual set of *Noruz* clothes, the tailor knew without having to ask who was getting married and who had passed away. Her mother never grieved or ate alone. There was always family to share what life offered. Tayebeh's knowledge was derived from the senses, rather than from books. For maladies of the body, she had an herbal mix. For those of the heart, a poem or proverb. Akhtar concludes that these days, the scales of contentment lean in her mother's favor. Toward her mother's simple life.

Akhtar speaks softly into the mouthpiece. From the other room, Reza listens to their every word. "Will Hadi and the kids be coming, too, this weekend?" She asks her daughter.

Akhtar's daughter married an Iranian man, Hadi. She had assumed—and braced herself—that her daughter would eventually marry an American boy, not an Iranian. But the man her daughter chose nevertheless shook Reza to his core, a boy whose background stood for everything that Reza was against. By marrying Hadi, her daughter had challenged Reza to a duel. It seems to Akhtar that they always had a battle of wills. From day one.

"*Chi?* What's that you say? You want to write about us? Our life story?" Akhtar asks, surprised by the seriousness of her daughter's tone. It seems she wants Akhtar to discuss something with Reza.

Akhtar hangs up the phone, says a prayer, as she always does after their conversations, and heads back toward the garage.

"What were you talking about?" Reza asks as she passes the living room.

"She wants us to consider something."

"What's that?"

"She wants to tell our story."

"What story?" Reza asks, perplexed.

"Our story. Why we're leaving, why we came, what happened in the years in between. She wants our permission."

"Permission for what?"

"I already told you, to write our story! She's still upset that we're leaving. She wants to write things down . . ."

Akhtar looks at Reza, slumped in his yellow chair, his hair disheveled, his bifocals riding half-way down his nose, his hands trembling violently, files scattered about his feet. Still, one look at his face and she knows he is more than pleased.

"I have a lot of stories to tell her! She'll want to know how I started working for NIOC. It was December 21, 1946. *Shab Yalda,* winter solstice. I still remember the date as if it were yesterday!" he says excitedly, realizing that Parkinson's hasn't stolen his memories . . . not yet.

"You've already told those stories a million times. I'm sure she knows them by heart. I have to get back to work," she says, not surprised that her husband immediately assumed that *their* life story only consists of his. *Maybe it has,* she thinks cynically as she walks down the vestibule steps.

Back in the garage, Akhtar straightens a garbage bin, resuming the seemingly never-ending task of moving and emptying boxes. Shifting things to and fro, she thinks about the telephone conversation she just had with her daughter. Isn't ironic, she contemplates, that the child she nearly aborted—the nearly erased life—is the one who wishes to document her life? Her daughter's interest, she assumes, stems from her overly sentimental ways, a characteristic often derided by her brothers.

So different is her daughter from her two sons that Akhtar often questions whether the three siblings share the same blood.

Had she gone through the procedure with Dr. Jandaghi, she shudders to think, she would have deprived herself of the deepest bond she's known. How close she came to losing her daughter and what a mistake that would have been. These nightmares still haunt her.

In 1975, when her daughter was thirteen years old, Akhtar ran into Dr. Jandaghi at a dinner party in Washington, D.C. It was hosted by a famously rich member of the Iranian expatriate community. She and Reza, with their daughter, had traveled to Washington for the occasion. Dr. Jandaghi, she came to learn that evening, had set up his medical practice in the area and was close friends with the host.

Akhtar was standing next to an overly stuffed buffet table with her daughter at her side, marveling over a champagne and caviar display, when Dr. Jandaghi walked toward them. It was such a surprise to see him that Akhtar gasped. He'd grown slightly heavier in the years that had passed, and white hair shimmered like strands of silver in his sideburns. To Akhtar, who had not seen him since that decisive appointment, he appeared as angelic as he had at their last encounter. He stopped and smiled. She could smell his expensive cologne, mixed with tobacco and alcohol.

"Akhtar *Khanom*," he said, astonished. "Is this," pausing to look at her daughter, "who I think it is?" Dr. Jandaghi then beamed with a delight only Akhtar could appreciate.

Without so much as waiting for an answer, the likeness making it obvious, he locked her daughter in an embrace. Akhtar saw that it was done with genuine warmth.

"You must be pleased with your decision, Akhtar *Khanom*," were the only words he had for that long-gone day, recognizing that the topic, like a rose with thorns, should be regarded but not touched. That night they talked briefly, a polite exchange suitable for the party.

More recently, Akhtar had learned through the family grapevine that Dr. Jandaghi passed away unexpectedly. He had died alone, a recluse in many ways, having been abandoned by family and friends. Apparently he'd been drinking heavily and had lost his medical license. Akhtar believes he'd gone wayward because he had not been cut out for his profession—perhaps he had waged a private moral battle. Her daughter reminded Akhtar that she's overlooking the fact that, after the Revolution, many in the elite Iranian expatriate community fell into severe mental depression. Dr. Jandaghi was of that class, so maybe what derailed him was the outcome of the Revolution, not a professional moral conflict. Whatever the cause, his death remains hard for Akhtar to accept. She is saddened that she had never truly conveyed her profound gratitude. Something tells her that maybe explicit words weren't needed.

"How would you describe your life?" her daughter had asked her over the phone. It was a good question, Akhtar had to admit. What *will* she tell her daughter when they sit down to talk? After a pause, she thinks, "This is it." She fans her arms around the garage, as a master of ceremonies would before its cast of actors. "Right here in these boxes is the story of my life in America." She points to the jumbled lot and smiles sadly.

"How do I sum up the contents of these boxes?" she asks herself. She realizes that to recall the events is one thing, but to string the memories together—to be the storyteller her daughter expects—is another. She knows the notes but not the tune. If there's a song to write, a life to sum up, her daughter will have to compose it.

Now she is curious to know which memories her daughter will want to reveal. Where in time should the narrative begin? Where to end? Whose accounts and which voices will she recall? What parts of their life's journey will she chronicle . . . which will she ignore?

Akhtar wonders if her daughter will include her own teenage years or gloss over them. Now, with a husband and two kids, her daughter wants to forget those years. To neatly tuck them behind a locked door. Of those years she keeps no photographs in sight, lest her children see the ghost that once haunted their mother. But Akhtar can never forget. For her it's an essential part of their story, of her story, of her lonely years in this country. Reza was back in Iran then, and Akhtar, a single mother in America. Those were the years when Akhtar needed the advice and support of relatives, of loved ones. Yet they were so far away that they never would have heard her screams of anguish. Akhtar was watching her daughter suffers but didn't have a clue how to save her or whom to turn to for help.

Bending to put a pile of books into a box, Akhtar stops for a moment to look at the eclectic assortment already lined up, cover-to-cover. Tightly jammed together are a Farsi-English dictionary, an Iranian cookbook, some storybooks once shelved in her daughter's room, and a colorful *Junior Encyclopedia Britannica* set that Reza had bought Keyhan in London. Along the far edge of the box, there are also some magazines, a year's subscription to *National Geographic* (a subscription gift from Reza's now-deceased American friend Allen), and a single copy of an October 1977 *Reader's Digest.* Pulling out the faded copy, Akhtar notices that a feature article, "Girl Who Wouldn't Grow Up"—the one she had read numerous times—still remains earmarked. She doesn't know how she came to have this copy of *Reader's Digest*, but she remembers that it landed in their mailbox at that desperate time when she needed to figure out what ailed her daughter. It was as if the complimentary copy of the *Digest* magically appeared in their mailbox so that she'd know what her daughter was going through. When Akhtar first read the article, she thought the author was describing *her* daughter. She didn't realize that her daughter's symptoms were shared by a growing population of adolescent girls. It had been eye opening. Akhtar read the article over and over again. Even with her slow English, she hadn't skipped a word—not even a vowel. Though it contained neither hope nor remedy, it enlightened Akhtar about the crisis facing them. Once she'd figured out what the demon was, Akhtar had stood vigil until her daughter was safely back.

Akhtar fans through the pages of the article. She turns once again to the first page to look at the hyphenated word that finally gave a name to the leech sucking the life out of her daughter: anorexia-nervosa.

With her broken English, it had sounded as daunting as the task of bringing her daughter back.

Akhtar crouches down and sits on one of the steadier boxes in the garage. The sight, or mention, of that word still steals her breath away. Leaning forward to rest her elbows on her thighs, still fidgeting with the *Reader's Digest,* Akhtar remembers the loneliness she experienced during that time. She sighs deeply. She thinks that it was perhaps the only time in her life that she had assumed the role of a fighter, willing to shout and yell in order to get her daughter back from the grip of death.

It had taken every ounce of Akhtar's energy not to look at her daughter and cry, though she did, privately, several times a day. At night, when she was alone in bed. In the shower, her cries mingling with the sound of water. After breakfast, when her daughter left for school without having a morsel of food. She remembers holding her daughter tightly by her frail shoulders and looking imploringly into her eyes, begging her to stop this hunger strike. She pleaded and pleaded with her, asking what it was that she had done to deserve a child who was starving herself to death. Was it her punishment, she'd wailed to God, for wanting to get rid of her fetus? Surely, her guilt told her, it was the price to be paid for something *she* had done wrong.

Her daughter spent most of her time in her room. Akhtar would peer in. She could see the shaggy blue carpet, stained and worn, installed by the previous owners. On a white dresser were stuffed animals and a radio, above it, on a cork board, carefully pinned photographs of Keyhan and Kambiz. Only a few feet separated them, from the door to where her daughter sat. Two steps at the most. Yet, the distance between them was a gulf. As though Akhtar were standing in her childhood house in Kerman while her daughter sat in her bedroom in America. Between them stood oceans and deserts, languages and cultures. A distance that, with each passing day, with each lost pound, kept widening. Akhtar found her daughter's American teenage world, including this disease it had given her, incomprehensible. She'd looked at her daughter's frighteningly skinny body and wondered how food had become her daughter's enemy. Standing a safe distance outside the room, she'd ask herself, "Doesn't she have everything in life that should make her happy? Didn't we come to America so that she would have a better life, the gift of opportunity?"

But, no matter how closely a mother watches her child, what can she truly see? How could she have missed this change in her daughter? When did it occur?

Was there a first time her daughter skipped the Basmati rice? Had she thought that her daughter just hadn't liked her cooking that night? Had there even been time to think?

Early in September of 1978, Reza called to tell Akhtar that he was coming to Rhode Island for a short break. "To weather the current unrest in Tehran," Reza had said, certain that he would not be staying long. Akhtar remembers that rather than feeling relieved, she had panicked. Her husband would not react calmly when he saw his daughter. He would blame Akhtar. Then she would have two fires to control—a furious husband and a stubborn daughter.

But Reza had mentioned that he first had to get a visa, *and* that NIOC was sending him to Egypt for a short-term assignment. This bought Akhtar time. Though not much. The clock was ticking, and she had a daughter to bring back from the depths of that disease.

Covering her face with her hands, she travels back . . . back toward the dark memories of that year.

* * *

On January 7 and 9 of 1978, in the city of Qom—a holy site to Shi'a Islam—four thousand religious students protested an article in the newspaper Ittila'at, in which the Shah's minister of information said that the Ayatollah Khomeini was a "traitor working with foreign enemies." Clerics and Islamic militants set up street barricades, smashed buses, halted trains, and attacked banks and shops. The police opened fire on the protesters. The shooting spree lasted two and a half hours. The government claimed there were between two and nine fatalities. The students claimed that seventy students—maybe more—were killed.

Shi'a tradition requires a commemoration forty days after a death. Religious leaders called for strikes on February 18, 1978. In response, the Shah decided that his government must control the streets of Iran. Security forces opened fire in Tabriz, killing as many as one hundred. The government acknowledged ten deaths. On March 30, forty days after the second attack, over one hundred protestors were killed in Yazd.

Demonstrations and protests against the Shah continued throughout the summer of 1978, throughout the forty-day Shi'a cycle of mourning. There were attacks on banks, luxury hotels, and government offices. Movie theaters also were set on fire. The movies were haram, forbidden, to the Shi'a clerics. They saw movies as anti-Islamic, Western propaganda that was destroying the purity of Islam in Iran.

* * *

On August 20, 1978, the Cinema Rex movie theater in Abadan was set on fire with hundreds of people inside. The exit doors were locked. Four to five hundred people burned to death. Who set the fire and exactly how many died in the blaze is still debated. The next day, ten thousand people gathered for a mass funeral in Abadan. The people in the streets blamed the Shah and his secret police, SAVAK. The Shah was losing control of the streets.

* * *

At the center of Tehran's bustling financial district stands a bearded and turbaned white-stone figure of Ferdowsi, the great Persian poet. Passersby can sense his greatness, even from a distance. To some, the statue seems austere. In his left hand Ferdowsi carries his national epic, the Book of Kings, and with his right he reaches forward in unbound determination. Since Ferdowsi's stories relate the history of old Persia, they tell of the glory of its kings from seven thousand years ago, well before Arab conquests introduced Islam to its people. Nestled at the foot of the statue, beside Ferdowsi, a childlike angel looks prophetically toward the future. Perhaps both angel and poet surmise that on this morning of September 9, 1978, the time has come for what could have been Ferdowsi's concluding chapter. One that he might title, "The Demise of the Iranian Monarchy." It would tell how the Persians finally succumb to Islam, surrendering culture and nationality to religion. A fourteen-hundred-year tug of war. A bitter end for some, an auspicious beginning for others.

Tehran
September 9, 1978

The street that passes through Tehran's Ferdowsi Square is
packed with people.

Reza steps out of the cool shade of the Bank Melli, past the
four pillars and the bronze lions guarding the central bank of
Iran. He shades his eyes from the bright mid-morning sun,
joining the din and traffic of in the Square. He lifts his Samsonite
briefcase to hail a cab.

A white Paykan, a small box-shaped car, pulls up. Nearly every
car in Tehran is a Paykan. The Shah hails Paykan as the
country's manufacturing pride and joy, but its operating license
and profits are held by the British company, Talbot. Like the
other manufacturers in Iran, the labor is Iranian, the owners are
foreign.

"*Koja agha?* Where to sir?" the tatty bearded driver asks in a
thick, provincial accent. He is in his twenties, wearing a loose,
collarless shirt that extends below his beltline. Though the shirt
is black, it fails to hide the stains. A photograph of Imam Ali, the
Prophet Muhammad's son-in-law and first disciple, a symbol of
Shi'ism, dangles from the rearview mirror. And his forehead,
framed in the rectangular mirror, bears a dark smudge from
placing his head on a prayer stone over and over again. His
prayer ritual has left its trace: the center eye, the mark of a
devout Muslim.

Reza climbs onto the back seat. The cab reeks of old sweat.
The driver wears the look of a *mazahbi*—one of the faithful.
Mazhabi, Reza thinks to himself, slovenly idiots who know
nothing about basic hygiene. Islam tells them to wash their hands
and feet before prayer, and that's their idea of cleanliness.
Religion is to blame for their backwardness, Reza thinks. Here is
just another person from the slums of Tehran, where life is bleak
and crime is high. These people come from all over to find jobs
in this great city, but they end up ruining it instead. Besides their
neighborhood mosques, they have nowhere else to go, and so

they bring filth to where *we* live. Reza cannot stand his type. If they weren't so lazy they'd get somewhere in life.

Reza's cologne soon overpowers the claustrophobic space of the cab. Disdainfully he gives the driver the address: "Kheyaban-e Farahabad." He shifts himself in the seat to straighten the back of his suit jacket, trying to avoid wrinkling. His neatly shaven face is reflected back to him in the side window. His image pleases him. It disappears when he rolls the window down to observe the frenzy of activity on the sidewalks.

"That street's closed, agha," the driver says dryly. He turns up the volume of his cassette player. A high-pitched cry of religious prayer pierces from the front speaker. It's agonizing for Reza to listen to it. Why would a young man listen to prayer over music?

"Turn off that racket!" Reza says. "Don't you have some music to play?"

Reza doesn't realize that this young man has been taught that music weakens the moral fiber. The driver learned that at the local mosque from a big-bellied, soft-skinned cleric. He goes to the mosque every night and sits shoulder to shoulder with other men, all packed in like sardines. He learned there that music harms the soul, that it breaks a faithful Muslim's trance with God.

Reza doesn't know that for the driver and other poor people like him, the clerics are the only source of education—and a decent meal. After prayers, they receive a free meal and the teachings of an exiled cleric named Khomeini at the mosque. The cleric sits at the head of the dinner *sofreh,* setting, and gets the biggest portion of meat. His double chin wobbles as he lectures. He tells the men that their minds should be filled with prayer. Then he passes out cassettes with recorded prayers, taped sermons by Khomeini, and flyers to post. In the driver's neighborhood, everyone is secretly listening to and then passing the tapes around. It's all they talk about.

The driver obeys Reza's command and turns the prayer tape off. He defers to this snooty, upper-class man, keeping each of them in their place. Why would he, simple and poor, have a music cassette to listen to? What in his life sounds like a melody? He says nothing to Reza, but mutters "*Allahu Akbar*" to himself. In the shuffle of life, kicks and blows come from above. You can't kick back from the bottom rung. One day his class will rise—this is what they say at the mosque. One day soon.

"And why is Farahabad Street closed?" Reza asks the driver.

"It's been closed since yesterday's event."

"What happened yesterday?" Reza asks, not sure he wants to know. Disturbing events have been springing up all over the country in the last few months. Naturally, the disturbance will end when the government takes control. How long can it take to subdue a handful of dissident clerics and their ragtag followers? He is at peace because most of the events have occurred outside of Tehran. For him, 1978 has been business as usual.

Reza is not alone in thinking so. He and his friends—secure and comfortable as they build their modern Iran—cannot understand why hundreds, even thousands, of Iranians are protesting the Shah. Even SAVAK—the Shah's secret police, who include informers and spies—does not know how widespread and well-orchestrated the protests are.

Reza reassures himself yet again. Shah is the mighty power of the Middle East. He stands shoulder to shoulder with the great Western rulers. A friend to America and Israel, countries that will protect him at all cost. Look at what happened in 1953, he tells himself. The CIA, under orders from President Eisenhower, staged a coup to restore the Shah to power. All power flows from him and his power is indestructible. Reza is confident that the *Shahanshah,* king of all kings, is powerful and invincible. He has kissed the ring of the great leader who made his career and life possible.

Reza has his job to do. Everyone has this job: stay loyal. SAVAK will take care of this mess—it's their job. Reza doesn't know—or even wants to know—how SAVAK is doing its job. SAVAK is in the good hands of General Moghadam, a family friend and the father of Keyhan's best friend. The General's three sons have spent nearly every day of the past six years with Kambiz and Keyhan. The General is a good family man. Just like Reza.

Reza dismisses the rumors. He has no knowledge of the corpses flowing into morgues—those killed by having broken bottles shoved up their bottoms, electric wires hung around their genitals, or poison sprayed into their eyes.

"What happened yesterday that they need to close the streets down?" Reza asks again.

Shocked, the cab driver turns to get a clear look at Reza. Everyone in Tehran must know by now. How could this man be unaware?

"Agha, three thousand of your fellow countrymen were killed by the hands of the Shah's army at Zhaleh Square!" he blurts out.

Reza looks out the window and says nothing.

"Three thousand peaceful demonstrators!" the driver says again, clicking his tongue several times.

"I wouldn't believe the rumors on the street if I were you," Reza finally responds.

"It was a massacre! The soldiers—down on one knee—rifles pointing at the crowd—they fired—point blank—the bodies fell, like a sickle through wheat—blood everywhere, people screaming, dying. Three thousand dead," the driver says again, the veins on his neck protruding.

"They had no business demonstrating. The authorities told them to disperse. You don't know. Just drive me to Ghandi Street."

"Agha, we want to take our country back! The Shah's a puppet. The foreign dogs pull him by a string. They have him by the balls. He's sold us out, like all our other monarchs. The people must be heard. You should listen to what mullahs are saying."

The driver turns to face the road. He has spoken his truth. He is shaking with vengeance. "Black Friday is what yesterday's being called."

"Black Friday, yellow Friday—can't you just step on it?"

The cab driver responds by slamming his palm against the gear stick. They slide into traffic and Reza catches a glimpse of Ferdowsi's statue as it slips from view. He takes a deep breath and assumes social order has been restored. For now . . .

A breeze brushes across his face as Reza leans back to look at the scenery of his cosmopolitan city. But today the scenery doesn't calm him. The words of the cab driver have alarmed him. The air in Tehran is suddenly brittle with hatred.

Reza now views things differently, clues that he had hitherto ignored: the broken windows of an English bookshop on Karim Khan Street, shattered bottles in front of the liquor store on Lalehzar Street, a barricade by Saedi Theater with a sign on it that says movies are profane and sinful. At the traffic light, Reza notices rows and rows of flyers posted on a brick wall. "Shariati" is written boldly across some, "Khomeini" across others. Some even bear the name of "Behrangi." The names are only vaguely familiar to him.

Reza has never read any of Shariati's widely disseminated publications. They are said to reveal Iran's social injustices, promote martyrdom, and call for a modern interpretation of religion in politics. Reza doesn't know that Shariati was recently assassinated in London and that his death sparked the first flickers of fire, mobilizing the religious community and bringing the exiled religious leader, Sayid Ruhullah Musavi Khomeini, to prominence. Reza doesn't know that Khomeini—first exiled to Najaf, Iraq, some fourteen years ago and this year to a suburb in Paris—is smuggling cassettes into the country.

Reza glances at the driver, who is rapping his index finger on the wheel, biding time. Reza senses that the driver knows something Reza does not, that in his world, the names of these leaders are as familiar as kin.

As they pass Shahreza Street, Reza notices several sanitation workers cleaning the sidewalk of debris. Behind them, a row of vandalized shops stands naked and vulnerable. Farther up, lampposts covered with flyers are being stripped clean by a group of uniformed soldiers.

Just past the soldiers, a kid no older than fifteen is being shoved behind a military truck. His hands are cuffed behind him, his face is bloody. When they pass Tehran University, Reza can see a line of soldiers with machine guns standing erect and tense. "DEATH TO THE SHAH" has been spray-painted on the stucco walls of the university.

Finally they arrive at Reza's modern apartment building. As Reza removes his wallet from the side pocket of his jacket, he finds his hands wet with perspiration. The cab driver hands him back his change, scowling. Then, staring directly into Reza's eyes, the driver flips on the prayer tape and puts it at full volume. He taps his finger on the steering wheel and speeds off.

The leafy neighborhood is quiet, idyllic. But Reza feels a pit in the bottom of his stomach. He needs a plan. At least temporarily—at least until things settle down.

Reza's mind begins to race. He has to figure out how much money they'll need, what to do with the apartment, how he will get another visa to the States.

The doorman always bows to Reza, a gesture Reza cherishes. It reminds Reza of his lofty station, of how far he has come.

Once again, the doorman, with his hands across his chest, bows reverently before him. Reza doesn't even see him.

Tehran
September 27, 1978

The unrest continues to escalate after Reza's eye-opening drive through the streets of Tehran. As he makes plans to get his family safely out of Iran, another family whose fate will one day mesh with his is making similar arrangements. But this family—provincial, poor, devout—can send only one family member to safety: Hadi, the boy who one day will marry Reza and Akhtar's daughter.

* * *

Panicked, Hadi wants to say to his father, "*Baba,* I've changed my mind. I don't want to leave." But he is unable to utter the words that are stuck in his throat. He simply can't raise his voice above his father's whispered prayer, much less above the frenzied noise of Mehrabad Airport. "Go in the hands of *Ali,* my son," his father says, holding a Koran above his son's head. His voice—steady and comforting—recites the verses of *Van Ye Kad.* Something keeps Hadi from telling his father how scared he feels. He knows that if he turns back, he'll shatter his old man's hopes. He also fears his father would become the butt of everyone's jokes. Hadi knows how much this trip means to his father. To buy his son a ticket, he has sold everything they own of value: a plot of land and two carpets. He knows that his father is tearing apart his most cherished possession, his greatest source of pride: his family. He knows that if he were to say that he'd had a change of heart, he'd disappoint his father. He would never be able to look him in the eye again.

Until they reached the airport, the notion of going to America was like a dream, conjured by a rural adolescent's frivolous sense of adventure. Then, in that delirious airport scene, Hadi grasped the depth of what was happening. He suddenly understands that besides some cash, which his mother had sewn into the seam of his underwear, he has only himself to rely on. He realizes he is leaving home. This hits him like a brick.

When he tears himself away from his parents' embrace, his heart pounds like an ominous drum. Yet he reveals neither dread nor doubt to his parents. For a 17-year-old, in fact, he seems almost stoic. He turns around one last time. Between hordes of people coming and going, through obstructed views, he catches a final glimpse of his parents. For their sake, he even forces a reassuring smile. He can tell that his father is still murmuring prayers and that his mother is weeping. He waves one last time and steps toward the gates, a ticket and a passport in one hand, and a battered brown piece of luggage filled with homemade clothing in the other. Swallowing the lump lodged in his throat, he makes himself a promise. He tells himself that one day he'll make them proud. With this final thought, he turns and hands the guard his plane ticket.

That was only a few hours ago. Now Hadi briefly stops fidgeting in his crammed seat and cocks his head to listen to the announcement. *"Khanooman va aghayan,* ladies and gentleman," the pilot announces over the intercom in a muffled voice, barely audible over the noise of the main cabin.

"Our altitude is thirty-thousand feet and the current temperature outside is negative thirty Celsius."

This IranAir flight on September 27, like others leaving the country following the political turmoil of Bloody Friday, stirs with discernable tension. The anxiety is in many ways the same, and in many ways different, from the panic running through Hadi's veins.

"Our estimated time of arrival . . ."

Hadi tightly knots his fingers together and peeks through the plane's bubble window. All he can see are clouds, Tehran's skyline having long since vanished from sight. As he gazes across the white blanket of moisture with its seemingly endless horizon, he tries to gain control of his emotions.

Boxed in his seat, with near-feverish alarm, he tells himself over and over again, "It's really true. I'm going to America. This is *really* happening."

It had happened so fast from the moment his father gave him the news to this flight: three months and seven days, to be exact.

Word got out in the neighborhood immediately. People could not believe that Ahmad Khalili, Dervish by belief, teacher by profession, from the village of Shavarin—a devout and simple man whose modest means could only afford him a two-room house of sun-dried brick—was sending his son to America. There was so much commotion in the neighborhood that Hadi simply didn't have the opportunity to reflect on the abrupt turn of events.

"*B'emrica?* To America!" people would mutter incredulously. They couldn't believe that such an ordinary kid would have the good fortune of being sent abroad. Overnight, news of his impending departure changed things for Hadi. People began to treat him differently. Before he was like any other soccer-kicking punk in the neighborhood, wearing rubber shoes and tattered pants. After the news, Hadi became the neighborhood celebrity. People would stop him to shake his hand and wish him luck. His eighth-grade teacher, Aghay-e Akbari, who had frequently punished Hadi for making a ruckus in class and would drag him by his earlobe to the front of the room until his eyes welled up with water, had hugged Hadi as if he were a hero. Others clapped him on the back and flashed big grins.

Hadi had always associated *Emrica* with Iran's rich families. It was a place for city types, not for a *shahrestooni*—one from the province. His notions of America derived from imported dubbed television programs: *Charlie's Angels*, *Streets of San Francisco*, *Ironside*. And it was only rarely that he saw even these, when he visited relatives who owned TV sets.

The illuminated no-smoking and seatbelt signs blink off. The gentle sound of violins streams through the cabin intercom. Some passengers rise from their seats, others unbuckle their seatbelt clasps but remain seated. Hadi scans the cabin. The man next to him, older by at least two decades, pushes his chair back, lights a cigarette, and inhales deeply. With each rise of hand to lip, a waft of smoke travels over to Hadi before rising up in the cabin. As he breathes in the smell of burning tobacco, Hadi remembers the times he and his friends pooled coins to buy a pack of cigarettes. They had furtively smoked them in an abandoned building behind the old bazaar, far away from the disapproving eyes of their parents. It was forbidden, but thrilling. They acted like adults, puffing proudly, chasing away the dull days of village life. If his father had ever caught him smoking, he'd have whacked Hadi across the head with his *tasbih* beads, pulled him home by his earlobe, and given him a good lashing with his belt.

Now, as he breathes in the scent of tobacco from the man sitting next to him, he realizes he can light one anytime he chooses. His actions from here onward are his and his alone. A novel sense washes over him and relieves some of his earlier anxiety. He looks at the man's lit cigarette in contemplation, wondering whether he should ask him for a smoke. A devilish voice inside reminds him of his newly acquired independence. "You're free to do what you want," it tells him. "Go ahead and ask him for a cigarette!" For a few seconds, Hadi grapples with the benign but to him slightly sinister choice. Then he remembers the promise he'd made in the airport and refrains. Instead, he turns his gaze back toward his bubble window and stares outside at the endless stretch of darkening sky.

"Please observe the seatbelt sign . . ."

On the horizon's edge, Hadi sees deep colors of blue and purple emerging. Twinkling here and there, stars begin to reveal their magic. Along the span of the plane's wing, red lights flicker. It all seems so beautiful to him, this modern piece of machinery sailing across the earth's outer rim, gliding atop an expanse so wide that his eyes still cannot accept it. He wishes his brothers, Mehdi and Hamid, could be there with him to share this view. He knows how much they would enjoy seeing the world from this far up. He imagines what each would say. Mehdi, two years older and a voracious reader, would probably philosophize about the journey. He might quote Khayyam or Hafez, the poets he idolizes and whose works he continues laboriously to memorize. Or, because of his recent interest in Stalin and Lenin, perhaps he would interpret the experience from a communist slant, just as he did the anti-Shah protest meetings they used to attend together. At those mujahidin meetings, Mehdi would be filled with bravado and idealism, orating poetic but politically incendiary verses. On this plane, he would have probably drummed up something like, "The plane is a vehicle for the elite while the masses cling to the earth." Hadi smiles to himself. No doubt, he thinks to himself, Mehdi would have seen this plane ride through the rose-colored but cracked glass of politics.

Hadi smiles a sad smile. Oh how he misses them! he thinks. The notion of home is already tinged with pain.

Then, exacerbating the pain, he thinks of Hamid—his younger brother by two years. Hamid would have come up with something mischievous. He'd want to play a trick or meddle with some forbidden buttons.

Touching . . .

On this thought, Hadi's mind stops. A memory washes over him with a jab of pain. If only his brother had been more cautious. Inhaling deeply, as if he were taking a drag from the cigarette of the man sitting next to him, he lets his mind wander to Hamid.

"Hadi! You have an exam tomorrow. Go inside and study!"

"Moman, one more minute. I have to teach Hamid a lesson. He can't beat me in soccer," Hadi says, doing a trick move with the soccer ball.

"Hamid, go get me some bread. The sang-aky *will close in a few minutes. Never mind your senseless brother. Hurry."* That *said, she points her hand to send Hadi in to study.*

It is the end of the school term, during Hadi's tenth-grade finals. Hamid smirks at Hadi, gloating, as if he'd won something. Hamid could do no wrong in the eyes of his parents. He is their favorite. He does as he pleases, stirring up mischief. He causes trouble, but, unlike Hadi, Hamid never feels the sting of tasbih beads or the lash of his father's belt. So, Hamid laughs as Hadi goes inside.

Inside, Hadi has just opened his book when the shrill scream pierces through the house. Hamid! Then, a second scream—his mother. Hadi hears his father's footsteps rushing outside. He hears him yelling his brother's name. The call stretches like an echo down a well's chamber. Hadi runs outside to see what has happened.

In the courtyard, he sees his mother kneeling. Flagellating. Hard strikes across her head. By the wading pool he saw his father holding Hamid. Hamid's head is on his father's lap. His brother lies listless, skin singed. Hadi sees his brother's body suddenly tremble from head to foot. And then he is still.

Within reach of Hamid's body lies a bare electric wire. Like a snake that has struck, the murderer and its victim rest side-by-side.

From the aisle, a flight attendant waves to gain Hadi's attention. Hadi is not sure how long she's been standing there, but both she and the man beside him are trying to get him to open his food tray. Distracted from his thoughts, he clumsily toys with the clip and a tray falls into his lap. The attendant smiles, passes him his meal, and moves to the next row. Hadi looks under the sealed package. It looks and smells awful. He wishes his mother had packed him one of her spicy, fragrant meals. Feeling a pang of homesickness, he closes the flap. Staring blankly ahead, he goes back to his thoughts . . . to Hamid . . . and to how this idea of going to America was born.

*   *   *

In the days that follow, the house is heavy with grief. Somber and silent. Hamid's giddy laughter is gone. Hadi and Medhi tiptoe around the fragile silence. No one utters Hamid's name.

Hadi cannot pass the courtyard without feeling a chill crawl up his spine. Finally, he stops walking by it. He and Mehdi begin to spend all their time away from home.

Several nights a week, they attend religious lectures in the mosque near the central bazaar of Hamedan.They sit in the front row and are so faithful in attendance that the mullah knows them by name. They become the mullah's favorites.After his lectures, they sit by his side for further conversation. Hadi and Mehdi become his soldiers.They start to follow the mullah blindly.

The world is churning before their eyes. The mujahidin mullahs of Hamedan are preaching revolution in secret meetings and then in street protests. There are protests all across the country—in Qom, Tabriz, and Yazd. Hadi and Mehdi have grief in their hearts, and now the mullahs show them how to use their grief to right the world.

By day, Hadi and Mehdi distribute the cassettes and newsletters of Ayatollah Khomeini; by night they attend the meetings held in the mosque by the central bazaar. They keep their eyes open, take secret routes, and develop hiding places. They have to be careful, for SAVAK, the Shah's secret police, could be anywhere and everywhere.

In the heart of his grief, Hadi feels an odd sense of exhilaration—like an elaborate game of hide and seek, like the thrill of sneaking a cigarette. He and Mehdi have become devoted revolutionaries and keepers of secrets. They learn on the streets where the secret meeting will be each night, sometimes only an hour or two beforehand.

Then, on May 19, 1978, 16-year-old Hadi hears that the cleric Sheikh Ghaffari will give a sermon that night. Sheikh Ghaffari is known for his sharp attacks on the Shah and has earned a following among the young mujahidin of Hamedan. It is only a rumor, no one knows where or when the Sheikh will speak. Hadi senses the excitement on the streets.

At dusk, Hadi and Mehdi receive word: the old mosque—Masjid Jameh—near the center of town.By 9 PM, inside the outer wall, the courtyard of the mosque is full. Several hundred faithful kneel to hear the Sheikh. Some are praying, lowering their heads to the prayer stone, their foreheads etched with the central eye of the devout.On the tops of the courtyard walls policemen stand, brandishing guns. From the top of the wall, the crowd must look like sheep crammed into a pen.

Sheikh Ghaffari unleashes his fiery rhetoric. He condemns the Shah and the creeping sickness of the West as it seeps into Iran. He promotes Khomeini and his promises of an Islamic nation. He rails against liquor, movies, and the Westernization of Iran by the Shah. The Shah is keeping each man here in the courtyard in poverty and misery, and he keeps each man from Allah and the path of righteousness. The Shah is a monster.

Mehdi nudges Hadi and whispers the Ferdowsi poem:

A monster fell, of a dusky hue,
And eyes that flashed with hellish glow;
Many it maimed and some it slew,
The back to the forest again it flew,
As an arrow leaves the bow.

The monster must be slain. Suddenly, the lights flicker and Sheikh Ghaffari vanishes. In the darkness, Hadi sees a flame burst forth. The cry rises, "Death to the Shah!" Near the front, two men jostle an effigy of the Shah on a broomstick. "Death to the Shah" echoes again and again and the effigy bursts into flame. The crowd roars like a vengeful lion. Then, out of the roar, gunshots burst the air. Police snipers are firing into the crowd from all directions.

Hadi and Mehdi flee, with a stampede at their heels and bullets over their heads. Outside the mosque, three men grab Mehdi, pull his shirt up over his head, and beat him with rubber batons and fists. Hadi pushes back to find his brother, but he is swept away by the crowd.

There are screams of agony, feet pounding against the stone, and gunshots exploding.

Hadi tries to melt into the crowd, looking for Mehdi. He tries to circle around, but the crowd is spinning out of control. He screams Mehdi's name . . . tears roll down his cheeks. There is blood on his shirt . . . but from where?

He makes his way to one of their hideouts—a kharabeh, an abandoned building—where he collapses, sobbing. How long does he wait? He doesn't know, but he hears a door open. Terrified, he looks for a weapon. Then he hears Mehdi's voice, "Hadi, they got me."

They make it home well after midnight. They can still hear yelling and gunshots in the distance. They are both bloody—Mehdi from his beating, Hadi from some unknown victim.

Their father is awake and waiting. He sits cross-legged under a fluorescent lamp with his Koran open in his hand. Tiny seeds of sweat glisten on his forehead. He looks pale, and struggles to restrain a great anger—or perhaps a greater sorrow. He has never looked so stricken. Not even at the death of Hamid.

Hadi and Mehdi stand at the threshold, unsure. They are both breathing heavily. Finally, Ahmad motions them to the ground. With heads bowed, in reverence and in shame, they kneel before their father, waiting.

His deep voice quavers as he fights to keep his composure.

"May you never feel the pain of losing a child. Spare your mother and me from burying another."

Ahmad says no more that night. They sit together—a father and his two remaining sons—in silence, until all the sounds of the night die away and the sun begins to rise. Only then does Ahmad nod his head to release the brothers to sleep.

Ahmad keeps his silence the next day.

Two days later, as they sit around the lunch sofreh, Ahmad turns to Mehdi and says, "Son, you will go to Emrica."

There is no explanation, no comment. It is as if he had told his son to go next door to borrow milk.

The long hours of silence have stiffened Mehdi's resolve. He has deeply considered his duties and they stand clear in his mind.

"I cannot," he says. Ahmad is stunned.

"I have come too far in this Revolution," Mehdi continues. "I have worked too hard for my people. I cannot walk away."

Ahmad studies his son's face as if he sees something for the first time. A son does not refuse his father. And then: "Baba, may I go?"

It is Hadi. He says it without thinking, as if he just wants his father to know he is there. He is not the son who memorizes poetry. He is not the youngest child who brought simple joy to his father. He has lived under two shadows. Let a light fall on him.

For the second time, Ahmad looks at one of his sons as if he doesn't know him. As he considers Hadi, he holds back a slight smile and then gently nods his head. "Yes, Hadi, you may go."

* * *

"Ladies and gentleman, we've begun our descent into London's Heathrow airport . . ."

Hadi starts to feel weary all over again. They are about to land. From London, he still has another flight to take to New York and yet another to Boston. Tired and worried, he glances once again out his window. This time he notices large areas of deep green landscapes. Nothing like the yellows and browns he'd left behind when they took off from Mehrabad Airport. As the plane drops altitude, he can spot tiny row houses, multi-lane highways with fast-moving cars, and neatly spaced streetlights—all new vistas for Hadi.

There will be no one to meet him in the States. Hadi knows no one in America. He has only the address of the school that gave him his student visa. That school, he understands, is on a street called "Boylston" in Boston. Hadi has no idea how to get there. For the time being, he'll worry about finding his next flight.

As he buckles his seatbelt, he murmurs a prayer. The same one his father read for him back in Tehran. Then he holds his breath and waits for the plane to hit the ground. With a thump so forceful that Hadi will never forget it, the plane's landing jolts him into an entirely new world.

* * *

By November of 1978, labor strikes protesting the Shah's government have begun to cripple the Iranian economy. Oil production—the life blood of Iran—has dropped from its peak of 5.8 million to below 2 million barrels a day.

The Shah installs a military government on November 6. The military immediately imposes a national curfew, which is widely, and brazenly, ignored.

On November 23, Ayatollah Khomeini—from exile in France—issues a declaration calling for national protests during the sacred month of Muharram, the first month of the Islamic New Year. Khomeini's words are recorded and distributed throughout the mosques of Iran.

Khomeini's declaration combines the traditional public processions of mourning during Muharram and a call for continued protest. He calls it, "Muharram: The Triumph of Blood Over the Sword":

> *With the approach of Muharram, we are about to begin the epic month of heroism and self-sacrifice, the month in which blood triumphed over the sword, the month in which truth condemned falsehood for all eternity and branded the mark of disgrace upon the forehead of all oppressors and Satanic governments, the month that has*

taught successive generations throughout history the path of victory over the dagger.

For Reza, these protests not only attack the great leader of his country, but also threaten to destroy his company, his career, and the purpose of his life.

Narragansett
1978

Just a few days short of Thanksgiving, Reza calls to say that he
has gotten his visa and will be home in a couple of weeks.
Akhtar feels her heart sink.

In Narragansett, the air is chilly and gray that Thanksgiving.
This is Akhtar's favorite American holiday—a celebration of
gratitude. Her father, Sadegh, had always taught her to be
grateful to Allah for her blessings. But this year she wonders
what there is to be thankful for. Her husband and son are living
in a country wracked with violence. Kambiz is never home,
always hanging out with his Iranian friends. Her daughter is
starving herself to death.

Akhtar has decided to entice her daughter to eat before her
husband's return. She kisses the Koran that Sadegh had given
her and goes to work. She cooks a turkey and fills their oval
table as if expecting an army of guests. She puts out the fine
china and silverware she had bought in New York. She puts
extra saffron and butter on her Basmati rice, an aroma that could
entice the dead back to life. For dessert, she makes her
daughter's favorite: brownies.

As she cooks and stirs, Akhtar prays to the holy book and to
her father's soul that her daughter will eat that night. She kisses
the Koran over and over again.

But her daughter refuses to eat a morsel. The perfectly baked
golden bird sits on the oval kitchen table the entire night, with
Akhtar sitting alone beside it. Crying.

That night, Akhtar knocks gently on her daughter's bedroom
door. She enters and sits on the edge of the bed. Under the
covers, her daughter rolls over to face the wall.

"Give me your hand, *azizam*."

Akhtar fumbls for her daughter's hand under the covers.

Her daughter's face has sunk around her cheeks, and around
her eye sockets, even deeper. Her jet-black mane has lost its

sheen, it is dry as the bristles of a broom. Her once-rosy lips are chapped, her nails are cracked and yellowed.

Akhtar finds her daughter's hand. It is cold, like the metatarsals of Azrael, the angel of death. Akhtar turns sharply. Azrael is in the room—in the corner and ready to pounce!

Akhtar shivers. Fear grips her, cold fingers clutch her throat. She chokes hard.

With both hands—with all her strength, Akhtar pulls on her daughter's hand, rolling her over until she could see into the girl's hollow eyes.

She pulls her daughter tightly to her and tries to cry out. No words come.

"Moman, please! You're hurting me," she hears her daughter say.

Akhtar releases her.

The room feels ice cold. Then Akhtar starts speaking slowly, in Farsi. "Your grandmother was Tayebeh and my grandmother was Jan-Bibi. We lived in Kerman . . . They couldn't read, but I learned . . . I went to school . . . I remember her, my grandmother . . . in the courtyard . . . and the bread lady would come . . . and it smelled . . . so . . . good . . ."

And so it begins.

Each night, Akhtar sits on the edge of that bed, gently holding her daughter's hand and speaking in a soft voice about the women of Kerman and their families. And the courtyard, with its wading pools and chickens.

Her daughter hides her face. But Akhtar continues to say in Farsi everything that comes to her mind about her family—about pussy willow tea, about the faith of Sadegh, about sleeping on the roof under the stars on summer nights.

On a wintry December night, Reza arrives in Narragansett.

"Ungrateful! She is wretched—ungrateful! I pay for her American education and this is how she repays me. Does she hate me?

"You are her father."

"Can't she see what's happening? Iran is falling apart—people are dying—and she just gives up?"

"I can't explain it."

"How long has she been like this?"

"I don't know."

"You don't know—you don't know? How the hell can you *not* know? Where have you been?"

"I'm right here."

"Letting your own daughter starve to death."

"She is sick."

"Sick? She is not eating, that's not sick. Where did you get that—sick!"

"Please, Karbassi, she's not well."

"She's skinny and ugly—she looks like she will die at my feet."

"Try to understand—"

"Understand? Khanom, I'll tell you what I understand—I paid for this house, I sent you money to eat and take care of your children, and what have you done? Do you throw my money away? Do you save the money for the food she doesn't eat?

"No, Karbassi."

Reza grabs a cookbook from the kitchen shelf and throws it at the wall just over her head.

"No, Karbassi, don't—!"

Their daughter slips into the kitchen.

"Baba, no."

Reza stops to look at his daughter.

"Look at you—you're not a girl, you're a skeleton."

"It's not your life," the daughter says.

"Not my life? I made you, I paid for you—"

"You don't own me, I'm in charge of myself."

"Then eat some food!"

"I can't stand the sight of it."

"The sight of you disgusts me. Get out of here, get out of my sight."

Akhtar steps in between them.

"*Na*, Moman, don't—I don't care, Baba, I don't want to see you either. So, get out of *my* sight."

Reza sputters. His anger boils over. He grabs a kitchen chair, swings it over his head and shatters it against the wall. He shouts and yells until he is out of breath.

Late that night, Akhtar creeps quietly into her daughter's room again. She fumbles gently for her daughter's hand. This time, the hand stays put. Akhtar holds her daughter's hand, gently stroking her hair until long after she falls asleep.

An uneasy truce settles in after that. Reza and their daughter avoid being in the same room. Reza normally retreats to his yellow chair in the living room. Every day the situation in Iran changes, charged with rumors, accusations, tension, threats, and protests. Reza purchases a silver shortwave radio to monitor the news. His country seems ready to explode.

He listens to the daily broadcasts from Iran, but has no time to worry about the problems of his daughter. His daughter's problem seems pale to him compared to the happenings back home. He leaves their daughter alone. For this, Akhtar thanks Allah.

In the ensuing months, something occurs that Akhtar can really be thankful for: signs of improvement. Slowly, her daughter starts to eat. First a sip of milk, a crumb of brownie. Then a bit more. Although her daughter still counts calories with the preciseness of an accountant, meals become more regular and less of a battleground. The day her daughter reaches for a whole brownie, Akhtar rejoices inwardly.

* * *

On January 16, 1979, there comes the sudden news that the Shah is leaving Iran for "a personal vacation and medical reasons." On a red carpet stretched across the airport tarmac, the Shah salutes his top generals. His wife, Farah, is unable to control her anguish and cries desperately behind her stylish French sunglasses. In the days leading up to the Shah's departure, manufacturing strikes have paralyzed the nation. There are shortages of food and fuel, including heating oil. Oil production—the fount of Iran's exuberant wealth, crash modernization efforts, and heavy militarization—has become sporadic, such that oil already sold to the United States is being imported back to Iran at inflated prices.

Soon after the Shah's departure, an interim government led by the opposition leader, Shapour Bakhtiar, assumes control. Bakhtiar promises a constitutional government, and says the Shah will return as a symbolic monarch with a democratic parliament, like the British system. But in the chaotic days that ensue, Bakhtiar makes a miscalculated and insidious decision. Under pressure to appease the religious community, he rescinds Khomeini's exile decree, permitting the religious leader to return to Iran after fifteen years in exile. Bakhtiar is quoted as saying that he is allowing the highly popular cleric to return on the condition that Khomeini will stay out of the political realm. Bakhtiar wants Khomeini to create a Vatica style power structure in the city of Qom—in effect, separating religion and politics.

Three weeks later, on February 1, Khomeini lands on Iranian soil. He arrives by helicopter and lands at Behest-e-Zahra Cemetery, where he honors the martyrs of the Revolution. The welcoming crowd is euphoric, and so dense that there is nowhere for the helicopter to land. As the helicopter hovers, an ocean of people reach their hands to the sky, as if God himself were arriving. Khomeini's face is serene and calm as he looks down from the cockpit, one hand half-raised in blessing to the masses below him.

Within days of his arrival in Iran, Khomeini overthrows Bakhtiar's interim government and reveals that he has no intention of keeping religion separate from politics. In fact, he is about to use Islam as a means of gaining control.

On February 4, Khomeini appoints a prime minister, saying, "Since I have appointed him, he must be obeyed. The nation must obey him. This is not an ordinary government. It is a government based on the Shar'ia. Opposing this government *means opposing the Shar'ia of Islam . . . Revolt against God's government is a revolt against God. Revolt against God is blasphemy."*

Within days, street fighting breaks out between the Shah's Immortal Guards and pro-Khomeini rebel soldiers, known as the Homafaran—a secret society of lower-ranking air force and army officers who fought for the Revolution. The Immortal Guards are the elite of the Shah's Imperial Guard. They are selected through rigorous testing, including one that examines their ability to recite, by memory, their lineage back through twenty-three generations. Khomeini quickly declares a jihad, a holy war, on soldiers loyal to the Shah.

On February 9, at about 10 PM, the Immortal Guards begin their last stand. Meanwhile, revolutionaries and rebel soldiers have begun commandeering police stations and military installations, and distributing arms to the public. Finally, at 2 PM on February 11, in order to halt the bloodshed, the Supreme Military Council declares itself "neutral in the current political disputes." Revolutionaries quickly take control of government buildings, radio and TV stations, and the palaces of the Shah.

Halfway across the globe, Reza monitors every moment of the news from Iran over his shortwave. He is still stunned. How could there be so many of them, he keeps asking himself, where did all these people come from? It will end . . . soon. But instead he hears the daily chants:

"Allah Akbar, Khomeini rahbar, Allah Akbar Khomeini rahbar ... "
"God is Great, Khomeini is the leader . . ."

Narragansett
1979

Wind and rain slam against the narrow kitchen window. Akhtar can see nothing beyond—the world is pitch black this night. Bathed in the weak glow of the single kitchen light, she is filling her tea kettle, preparing for the nightly ordeal of the radio news from Iran. It is almost 9:30.

The family has gathered in the kitchen. The dinner dishes lie stacked and unwashed on the yellow Formica countertop. The silver shortwave radio sits at the center of the oval kitchen table—the table Reza bought as a symbol of modernity for his assimilated family. Reza sits closest to the radio, with Kambiz to his left and his daughter to his right. The broadcast is about to commence this night of April 11, 1979.

Then, two gongs chime the entry of the Voice of Iran announcer in Tehran:

This is the sound of the Islamic Republic of Iran, Besm Allah ElRahman ElRaheem. In the Name of Allah, the Gracious, the Merciful.

In the kitchen, it's as if time freezes. They all fall silent. Reza pushes the volume to its highest setting and tilts his head closer to the radio box. A door to Iran has opened.

Like the hapless gambler repeating the same bet each night, Reza continues to hope to hear that a coup has reinstalled the monarchy. But throughout the spring, the new revolutionary government under Khomeini has become stronger and stronger.

Today, the government announced that Khomeini's theologians' party is restoring order to the nation through its revolutionary cells. These groups have expedited the creation of local committees and are now called the Revolutionary Guards. They will run local governments across Iran.

"Propaganda," Reza huffs. "They claim triumph when it's pure anarchy. It's all hogwash, this Khomeini character . . ." he cuts himself short to hear the announcer.

. . . all national Bahá'í administrative structures have been banned . . .

Some of Reza's NIOC friends are Bahá'í. The announcer makes it sound almost innocuous. But Reza knows from the uncensored Iranian newspapers published in London that Khomeini's government has been destroying the holy places, shrines, and cemeteries of non-Muslims. Islamic doctrine declares that the Bahá'í's are heretics, and hundreds have already been summarily executed under Khomeini.

"Barbarians," Reza whispers.

The Rial is valued at 60 per American dollar.

"Did you hear that? Sixty!" Reza blurts out with anger. "Our money is devalued again. This is ten times what we were paying to convert money before the Revolution!"

As the exchange rate falls, more and more people in Iran convert their money to dollars to protect against the country's uncertain future. For Reza, it means that the money he saved in Iran is now worth approximately eleven cents on the dollar. He desperately needs money now, but he refuses to convert his savings accounts in Iran—the loss is too great. He'll wait until the Shah's government is back. That should be soon, he thinks . .

The broadcast continues for the next half-hour, running through the country's latest political and economic events. The last segment has become the hardest for Reza to listen to. Each broadcast ends with a list of people who—in Revolutionary rhetoric—have been "cleansed."

Today, the government commenced the executions of the former heads of the country's domestic security and intelligence service, SAVAK, dating back to the government organ's incipient 1957 date . . . General Nasser Moghadam, Nematollah Nassiri, and the institution's first director, Hassan Pakravah, were executed this morning in Tehran's Evin Prison.

The water on the stove begins to boil. A loud ghostly scream of steam pierces the silent kitchen. Rain continues to hammer on the kitchen window.

Kambiz drops the fork he has been playing with. Reza's hands begin to tremble. Akhtar stares straight ahead.

General Moghadam is not the first of their friends to be executed, but his death is deeply disturbing. Not only was he the father of Keyhan and Kambiz's best friends, he was also a protector of the family. If someone as powerful as General Moghadam can be executed, no one is safe.

Akhtar finds Reza's eyes and sees that they are both gripped by the same fear—Keyhan. Reza has asked Keyhan to leave Iran, to play it safe until things settle down. But, Keyhan, a staunch monarchist, refused. He didn't want to believe that the lavish dinners, fancy cars, parties at the American Club, or his beach vacations in Karaj could ever end.

Reza and Akhtar can see that Keyhan's circle of friends—all connected to the Shah's regime—have now become a noose closing in on Keyhan.

* * *

Since leaving Iran, the Shah has bounced from country to country—Egypt to Morocco to the Bahamas to Mexico. He suffers from gallstones and needs immediate surgery. Treatment is arranged in Switzerland, but the Shah insists on going to the United States for surgery. President Carter, at the personal request of David Rockefeller, allows the Shah to come to the States. The Shah arrives on October 22, 1979, ostensibly for a brief stay, but medical complications keep him in America for six weeks. Iran demands his extradition.

On November 4, in retaliation for America's protection of the Shah, a mob of several hundred students calling themselves the Muslim Students Following the Line of Imam Khomeini storm through the marine guards of the main U.S. embassy building. They seize control of American personnel. Sixty-six diplomats and staff are held hostage. Khomeini applauds the students' initiative and stands in allegiance with them against the United States.

The U.S. media begins tallying the days of the hostages' captivity. The animosity between the two nations grows with each passing day.

On December 15, 1979, Day 41 of what is now referred to as the Hostage Crisis, the Shah and his wife leave the United States for asylum on a tropical island off the coast of Panama. Within days, Iranian diplomats delivered a 450-page extradition demand to the Panamanian government. The Shah flees to Egypt, where he dies on July 27, 1980. Day 267. Egyptian President Anwar Sadat gives the Shah a state funeral. He is buried next to the last King of Egypt.

Boston
1979

By January, in the depth of a New England winter, Hadi is frozen out of his country. The airports are closed in Iran. Boston is battered by a stinging wind. On TV in Iran, America was portrayed as warm and blonde—*The Streets of San Francisco* and *Charlie's Angels.* In real life, Hadi finds his new environment icy and lonely, far from the images that he once associated with this country.

He attends Shaw Preparatory School in Boston, a makeshift diploma-granting institution that gave him his student visa. He has started to learn English. He'd learned some grammar in Iran, but he had never spoken English before reaching the U.S. Some people are patient when he speaks, but most are not. Now, in January, he is a 17-year-old boy, lost and confused, worried and uncertain. He is also in desperate need of money. The $3,300 that his mother had sewn into the seam of his underwear and the hundred dollars he had hidden in a belt is all but gone.

At Shaw Prep, someone tells Hadi about finding a job that pays cash under the table. By day he cleans toilets and washes dishes in a Boston restaurant. At night, during the graveyard shift, he pumps gas at a station in Roxbury. He rents a room over a Store 24 on Harvard Avenue in Brighton with two other Iranians he has met in Boston. The apartment has one window. It overlooks a dumpster in the alley.

Between the three, they have one mattress. They divide sleeping time into three shifts. Hadi has the morning shift because he works at the gas station until 6 AM. He buys cheap white bread and covers it with the ketchup, mustard, and mayonnaise from packets he pilfers from McDonald's and Burger King.

On top of all this, he still has to go to school.

In May, Hadi turns eighteen. School ends in June. He has no money to return home. And on November 4, when the Iranian students seize the American embassy in Tehran and hold sixty-six Americans hostage, hopes of returning home become even dimmer for Hadi. The United States breaks diplomatic relations with Iran. Along with hunger, exhaustion, and loneliness, Hadi now suffers an increasingly hostile environment.

Narragansett
1980

Reza is under siege. In the cold of winter, he has retreated to a small room of his house. The room is small, dark, and frigid—like an underground bunker, a frozen cave.

The thermostat is set to fifty-seven degrees to save money. The light bulb is a pale twenty-five watts, but it's turned off. The door is kept shut to retain any remnant of warmth.

Reza huddles in the dark under a scratchy woolen blanket, beside him is the shortwave radio. He rubs his hands together to stay warm. If there were a light, you would see a man physically withering before the chilly tides of the world. He has lost his distinguished businessman's gut—the mark of a man who does no manual labor—and his once jet-black hair is now gray. He is fifty-three years old.

His world has turned to ash. The value of the Rial has fallen further. But what does it matter? The Islamic government has frozen all his funds—they've done this to anyone living abroad. Reza's meager reserve of American dollars is slipping away, penny by penny.

The shortwave radio pops with static and echoes with chants of "*Marg bar Emrica . . . Marg bar Emrica*"—Death to America.

"Thank God for America," Reza thinks. It is his safe haven, a country founded on justice and freedom, a country that provides his kids with the finest education in the world. It is a country where immigrants of all nationalities have found shelter. It is a country that will accept him. All of this Reza knows to be true. He hopes, if they can hold out just a little while longer, that he can surface from his cave into the sunlight. As soon as he gets his immigration status worked out, he can emerge a new man, go to work, and begin to rebuild his life.

He keeps careful lists. The house and the car are paid for. He paid them off before the Revolution. There are utility bills—soaring because of the worldwide oil shortage. The thermostat barely keeps the pipes from freezing. There are grocery bills. He warns Akhtar over and over again, no frills, just enough to stay alive. There are property taxes. The government can take away your house if you don't pay your taxes.

He calculates the numbers again. The numbers don't change.

This is the sound of the Islamic Republic of Iran.
Allah Akbar . . . Khomeini rahbar . . .

Akhtar walks in carrying a tea tray and flips on the light. Reza glares at the open door and motions for her to be quiet—the news broadcast is about to begin. She quickly shuts the door behind her to conserve the heat.

She puts the tea tray in front of Reza and pulls up a chair.

In the name of the Allah, the gracious, the merciful . . .

The dim overhead light casts long shadows on both their faces. They look worn out, shoulders sagging under the weight of uncertainty. From under the blanket, Reza reaches one hand for his tea, stopping midway to listen to the voice of the announcer.

Today, the students at the American Embassy in Tehran
continued their demand that the American government
repatriate the deposed Shah to Iran to stand trial for his
decades of injustices.

It has been sixty-two days since November 4, the day the students seized the American embassy. Reza has followed every bit of news broadcast from Iran and in America.

On the American news broadcasts, Reza hears that the failure to resolve the hostage crisis has come to represent all America's problems and weaknesses: rising inflation, high interest rates, the loss in Viet Nam, crime rates, nuclear proliferation, immigrants, poverty, and pollution are all being wrapped up in this single, unifying national problem. They are not sixty-six hostages in a far away corner of the world: it is "AMERICA held hostage." Each day of captivity is marked off, as a prisoner does when marking the days in his cell: Day 7 of America Held Hostage . . . Day 35 . . . Day 44 and now . . . Day 62.

"How long?" is the question Reza asks himself every single day. How long can students defy the great world power of America? Every day American television shows mobs of bearded fanatics in front of the embassy, burning American flags and effigies of President Carter. They punch their fists in the air, shouting, "Death to America!" They hold signs in English saying, "Death to America." They don't understand English, but they do understand TV and they are prepared for their audience.

And, the audience in America is responding. Reza and Akhtar receive anonymous phone calls spewing curses and threats. Notes filled with profanity are stuffed into their mailbox. Their house is pelted with eggs. In December, Reza watches from his upstairs lair while Akhtar scrubs the hardened egg off the garage door, her knuckles raw in the icy air.

There is violence in the air—even in Narragansett. Although she would never tell her parents, their daughter has seen drunken college students chanting, "Fuck Iranians, Death to Iran." She doesn't need to tell them. They all feel it—like the strange pulsing of an approaching storm.

All Iranians are seen as violent, flag-burning zealots. Yet Reza—who has long admired the United States—shares the same contempt for Khomeini. After all, Khomeini is the one provoking the phone calls and the hate mail.

"Another day added to the countdown," Reza snorts angrily, abruptly lifting his tea off the tray. "How long will these idiots stand up to America?"

Ayatollah Khomeini calls the American government the Great Satan . . .

Taking a sip from her tea, Akhtar says, "Karbassi, that envelope looks important." She points to a stack of mail in front of Reza's feet. The envelope has the official American eagle seal on its corner.

"Something from INS," he says. He is waiting for a response from the Immigration and Naturalization Services to his request for legal residency. He taps the corner of the envelope, as he has always done since he started working for NIOC. He slides his finger under the letter flap. The letter is short, just a few sentences on heavy stock bearing the Great Seal of the United States. Reza drops the letter on his lap.

"Karbassi, *chi shodeh?* What's happened?"
He stares blankly at the white wall before him.
"Karbassi!" Akhtar repeats realizing the letter must be grave. "What does it say?"
"I don't know."
"Is it about the residency application?"
"There is nothing about our application in this letter."
"Then what does it say?"
He reaches over to the radio and turns it off.
"They're deporting us."
"Deporting us? But why? We haven't broken any laws."
"It says we have to leave—by March first."

Until now, Reza has never considered the possibility of deportation. He has thought of this country as a safe haven, a place out of harm's way. A land where immigrants of all nationalities have found shelter throughout the country's history. The lens through which he sees America still reflects a smiling Doris Day and Jack Lemmon, friendly and neighborly, a pristine image of America in the 1950s. Reza still maintains that this nation's education and legal systems are illustrious, particularly for those from a developing country like his. America is a nation that is fair and just. How can they send us back, with this political mess, with all the executions? Reza drops his head to his chest. He is scared and confused, uncertain about his family's future. He feels betrayed. The country he has held in such high esteem wants to force him out. "We haven't broken any laws," he tells himself. Why would they want to remove us? He asks himself these questions again and again, wringing his hands with worry. He's been a model citizen: always obedient, always respectful.

How can the legal guarantee of the American government be so easily nullified? Honor and trust are unquestionable in this exalted country. How can they—without warning—order him to be deported? He hasn't even had a hearing on his petition for residency. They haven't heard his side of the story. He has a right to a lawyer, doesn't he?

The bitter winter of 1980 wore on.

Reluctantly, with his last bit of savings, Reza hires an Irish lawyer from Boston. Mr. O'Neill is tall and well fed, with a milk white complexion and pudgy fingers. O'Neill looms over Reza, making Reza feel like he is shrinking under the pressure. Reza calls him "Sir" and bows to him. Mr. O'Neill spots a technicality in the government's letter to Reza, managing to delay the March 1 departure.

March 1—Day 123—comes and goes. Reza and Akhtar are still in the house. No one has come to deport them. But, as the hostage crisis drags on, the couple sense the venom flung at all "Eye—rain—ee—ans." He is treated as if, by virtue of his birth, he had caused the crisis. But rather than curse America for his problems, Reza continues to blame Khomeini and the radicals of the Revolution.

It is Day 173. April 24. Reza hears the story on his shortwave. The broadcast from Tehran claims that Iran had thwarted an American attempt to rescue the hostages.

"America—the Great Satan—has been beaten back. It is the will of God," the broadcast says.

"Propaganda," Reza says. "Lies."

So, he turns to the national news broadcast—the ABC Evening News with Peter Jennings.

* * *

Code-named Eagle Claw, eight helicopters attempted a bold rescue of the hostages held at the American embassy in Tehran today . . . Eight helicopters were sent to infiltrate Tehran over two nights . . . Two helicopters were lost in a sandstorm . . . One helicopter suffered mechanical failure and another lost control during takeoff. It crashed in an explosion of fire, killing eight American soldiers. The aircrew evacuated and left behind classified plans—documents that identify CIA agents in Iran.

* * *

Eagle Claw, Reza thinks, the symbol of American might. The claws that clutch both the olive branch of peace and the arrows of war on the Great Seal of the United States.

After Reza hears about the Eagle Claw operation, he realizes why he is being deported. The U.S. government is trying to deport as many Iranians as possible to avoid any backlash after a rescue. Had Reza contacted his old NIOC colleagues, he would have learned that they all faced similar situations. They were his friends. They were proud to work together, drinking fine Scotch over a table of Persian caviar. But he doesn't call. Long-distance phone calls are expensive. And, there is the inevitable question: How are you doing these days? Does Reza want to admit that he is unemployed, hiding out in a cold room, hoping for a miracle on his visa, and trying to survive as his life savings drain away?

The days wear on. The Hostage Crisis count continues. Reza either sits beside his shortwave radio on his yellow chair in the living room, scratching the back of his neck, or he carries the radio upstairs to the small room and sits alone in the dark.

Akhtar prays all day. Reza never tells her how much money they have, but he has told her that their savings are dwindling away. Without working papers and with their immigration status still up in the air, there isn't much they can do.

Day 192. The kitchen is filled with the rich aroma of fresh bread. Akhtar doesn't see her oven mitts, so she grabs a cotton towel to pull out the bread. Without thinking, she wraps the bread in the towel just as her daughter walks into the kitchen.

"Moman, what are you doing?"

"*Azizam*, I made brownies for you . . . see, there on the table. Get some milk."

Akhtar's daughter slides into a chair at the oval table. "But what are you doing?"

"Baking bread."

"I mean with the towel."

"I can't find my mitts."

"You wrapped the bread in the hand towel. I never saw you do that before."

"*No?* My daughter is telling me how to bake now?" Akhtar unwraps the loaf cooling on the oven sheet. "My own daughter—who won't let me teach her how to bake. Now you know everything?"

"I don't know . . . I just never saw you wrap it like that."

Akhtar checks on the bowl of rising dough. Her daughter shyly takes nibbles of the brownie. Out of the corner of her eye, Akhtar watches. She pretends to check on something else as she sees the nibble grow into a full bite. Akhtar has learned not to provoke a fight, but she is quietly celebrating another small victory: her daughter is eating.

"I guess I was thinking about Kerman," Akhtar says. "Jan-Bibi and I would wrap the hot bread in thick cloth."

"Did she teach you to bake?"

"No, I watched closely. I learned."

"But why do it here? This is America. You can buy perfectly good bread at the store."

"Your father—"

"Is too cheap to buy bread?!"

"*Azizam*—he will hear you." Akhtar motions for her daughter to lower her voice. "It's too soft here, the bread; too mushy he says. And, he wants to save money, it's true."

"Moman, please, this is America. Why are women forced to stay in the kitchen, chained to a stove? I can see making your own bread in Kerman, but here—"

"Ah, but we didn't bake our own bread. The baker lady came and we did it together."

"But you paid her."

"Of course we paid her. Two times a week. But she was our neighbor, our friend. She would talk with Jan-Bibi and my mother and brought all the news. She knew the gossip from every house. As long as I can remember, I sat with them by the heat of the tanoor oven—listening. Happy voices, conversations, bread."

"Well, there's no baker lady here. You should not do her job. Especially for free!"

"Not here. Here—no one talks to you, no one asks how you are. The bread is all the same and wrapped in plastic. You don't know who touched it and no good stories are baked with it. It's plain and lonely. Making bread should never be lonely."

Akhtar removes her Carnelian ring and her wedding ring. She sprinkles flour on the counter then on her hands and begins to knead the dough. Her daughter watches her strong hands dig into the dough, pull, fold, turn it, and then dig in again.

"Moman, you can be the baker lady here."

"I don't know anyone."

"Mrs. Etzel. She runs a coffee shop. I hang out there. All the foreign students go there. She could sell your bread there."

"I can't do that."

"Why not? You should sell your brownies and make cakes or something. You'll make money.

You'd like Mrs. Etzel. She's German, a widow."

"I don't know. I'll have to ask your father."

"No you don't have to!"

The International Coffee House at University of Rhode Island is small and cozy. There are overstuffed easy chairs, battered dining chairs beside castoff tables inside an old stone building. Mrs. Etzel always places fresh flowers on each table.

On her first day, Akhtar delivers four cakes to Mrs. Etzel for eight dollars each—thirty-two dollars cash. She takes her money and drives to Wakefield to buy more pans.

Each night after dinner, she sets up an assembly line. On the bright yellow Formica countertop, she piles bags of flour and sugar. She clears the oval table, greases her pans, and mixes all the batter by hand. It takes hours, but it saves the cost of electricity. In the morning, she drives to the coffee shop.

"Day 197 of America Held Hostage."

Akhtar sprinkles flour over the counter, getting ready to knead dough. She is half-listening to the television in the other room. She pulls her rings off one by one, placing them in the soap dish by the sink.

Reza groans from the other room as he heaves himself out of his yellow chair. He stands in the doorway of the kitchen watching her.

Akhtar pats her hands in flour and begins kneading—dig in, stretch, fold, pat down, and turn. She glances nervously at Reza. Her hands dig in, stretch, fold, pat down, and turn. She gently bites her lower lip.

Reza waits.

Soon she is in the rhythm of kneading.

Reza clears his throat sharply.

She stops. She turns to him. He looks angry.

Reza starts to speak, but stops.

"Karbassi . . .?" Akhtar says. She feels a sudden wave of sorrow for him. She has never asked for his permission to bake for money. She turns back to her dough. Her hands dig in, stretch, fold, pat down, and turn; dig in, stretch . . .

Reza's fury at Khomeini intensifies. Just like his grandfather Abolghassem's hate for the English and other foreign thieves, Reza's hate for Iran's new government swells. He thinks of them as thieves and foreigners. They cannot possibly be Iranian, he thinks. He hates the mullahs with their turbans, fat bellies, and filthy, sex-obsessed minds. They have turned the great country of Iran into a sewer of chaos, fear, and retaliation. All in the name of Allah. He promises himself that he will never cross paths with those vile creatures. In this life and beyond, he will never abide them or forgive them.

* * *

On September 22, 1980, Day 324, the Iraqi army invades Iran, pushing as far as the base of the Zagros Mountains. The war will eventually last eight years and cost more than half a million lives on both sides. Iran's clerics name the war the Holy Defense, and within months of the invasion drive the Iraqi army back to the border. As in World War I, there is trench warfare. Iran sends human waves of young men and boys over the trenches toward certain death and martyrdom. Iraq responds with mustard gas and machine gun fire.

Khomeini refuses to make peace, rejecting Saddam Hussein's offers of truce—597 of them. Khomeini declares that as long as Iran has boys who want a key to heaven—in other words, a steady supply of martyrs—the war will never end.

The Islamic government begins to crack down on dissent. They arrest members of the other political parties that helped in the Revolution. Hadi and his brother Mehdi were members of the mujahidin. Several of their high school friends are executed. Others are sent to prison. To dodge execution, Mehdi spends two years hiding in the mountains and later in his father's basement in Hamedan.

Boston
1980

Hadi calls home often. He spends precious money to make the calls from a phone booth. A full roll of quarters, ten dollars for three minutes.

"Baba, please let me come home. I'm very homesick."

"Pesaram, my son, if you come home now, you'll be immediately drafted."

"But I am miserable here, Baba. Please!"

"Hadi joon, they are sending young men to descend on enemy lines like swarming ants to be slaughtered. Young boys are being used to find landmines. For their heroic efforts they are given a plastic key and told that it opens the door to heaven. Is that where you want to end up?"

"But Baba . . ."

"I rather have a miserable and homesick child than a dead son."

Hadi continues to struggle on his own. No way to return home, no one to turn to. No legal papers to get a legitimate job. No way to go but forward, as he had once promised himself.

He could still hear the words of his father. "May you never feel the pain of losing a child. Spare your mother and me from burying another." Yes, he is not dead; he is not lost. But he is trapped in exile.

* * *

On January 20, 1981, Day 444, the American hostages held in Iran are finally freed. Twenty minutes after Reagan is sworn in as president, the ordeal that has haunted the United States comes to an end. The hostages first fly to Algeria: a symbolic gesture. It is only appropriate to acknowledge that government's role in resolving the conflict. After several intermediate stops, one of which is in Germany, where now-former president Carter greets them, the hostages are flown to New York City. There, along the Canyon of Heroes on lower Broadway, where the Financial District sits, the hostages are given a ticker-tape parade. The country is experiencing a surge of patriotism, the public mood needs to be displayed. This is a celebration of triumph, of America restoring itself once again to greatness. After all, the Iranians hadn't dared to harm any of their nationals. Their men are all back home. Safe.

Indeed, America has much to celebrate.

Chapter 10
Doors

Hadi, my husband, tells me that his last day in Iran was "life defining." He says that *that* particular moment was like opening a door, one of those which life rarely provides and behind which lies uncertainty. Neither he, waving his goodbyes nor his parents wiping their tears could have guessed how timely his departure was.

In May 2001, Ahmad Khalili passed away hours after our daughter, Donya, was born. Right to the very end, Hadi's father maintained that his son was lucky to leave Iran. Hadi is not so sure. Luck needs to be qualified, he says. To send a 16-year-old to the jaws of the unknown was simply a blind but optimistic risk on his father's part. Hadi also says—with the maturity and wisdom that come from hindsight—that if he had known he would be unable to return home, he wouldn't have left. But destiny, he adds, doesn't allow us to peek behind the doors we choose. And once we open a door, we can only let our guts chart the course and our brains manage the journey. That, he says, has been his way of surviving the difficult road he's traveled in America.

Narragansett
2005

In the garage, Akhtar finally snaps out of her reverie. Sliding the *Reader's Digest* back into the box, she rises from her spot to resume the tasks at hand, moving the batch of old books and magazines to the corner of the garage designated for recycling. For a brief moment, she stands—at attention—in front of the box, like a general honoring a soldier with a salute, a tribute to a momentous victory, a battle she'd like to forget but cannot.

They rarely talk about those days. Once her daughter mentioned how difficult it had been to fit in as a teenager in Narragansett. "They all thought I had come from a different planet," she said in describing those years. She had been the only "foreigner" at her school. The lone brown girl amongst the fair-skinned Narragansett girls. Her daughter tells Akhtar that her disease's psychological connection had to do with a sense of being different from the Americans. But Akhtar doesn't think so. She tends to think it's rooted in a father-daughter battle.

For years, Akhtar worried that the angel of death was keeping an eye on her daughter. For a while the girl routinely reverted back to her old ways of starvation. It was not until her daughter met Hadi that the grips of that awful disease finally seemed to wholly disappear. To this day, Akhtar thanks her son-in-law. "If it wasn't for you, Hadi" she tells him, "she'd sink again. And the next time, I fear I wouldn't have any more life in me to give her."

Turning on her heels to stride across the garage, Akhtar hears her mother's voice. From far deep in her heart, Tayebeh's mellifluous voice recites an old adage, as familiar to Akhtar as the wrinkles of her old hands. She remembers the strength she'd drawn from these words during those tough years with her daughter.

Dar na omidi basi omid ast.
In hopelessness there exists much hope.

Payan shab seyah sepid ast.
In the conclusion of a dark night there is light.

Those words helped sustain Akhtar when hope seemed faint. Lifting her head toward heaven, Akhtar says to Tayebeh, as undoubtedly her daughter will one day say to her, "Thank you, Mother. Thank you for helping me to persevere."

Narragansett
1984

Akhtar is standing on her Rhode Island lawn, breathing in the smell of fresh-mown grass wafting down the street. The lawns of Narragansett are green this spring, but it never seems quite right to her. Not like the deeper green that she expected to see in America. Not the same green as she had once seen in the photograph from her Uncle Khan Daee, the son of Haj Yazdi, who slipped away to America in the 1920s and became rich.

She remembers a riveting photograph—happy children, happy husband and wife, and a happy lawn—a deep green color available only in California, or in Kodachrome—she wasn't sure which.

Each spring she anticipates the greening of the lawns, just as she has sought the pussy willows growing along river banks. Each year she learns anew that the pussy willows of America have no fragrance and cannot make the delicate Iranian tea that she loves. And each year, she learns once again that the lawns of Narragansett can never be as green as the one in that photograph.

Khan Daee set a standard of green for Reza as well. Here was an Iranian man who, when still alive, fit into American society and beat them at their own game. He was rich. He wore a Rolcx watch and he drove a Jaguar. And he seemed impossibly happy.

Reza has been able to get the watch. But the Revolution stopped him from actualizing the rest of his dream. He still longs for the Jaguar . . . some day. For now his car is a used Toyota van, several years old, blue and dented. There are two seats at the front, and the back is clear for hauling and storing boxes for Dairy Mart.

Akhtar is waiting for Reza on the lawn. She is dressed up in a skirt and blouse. They are driving to Boston for dinner with their daughter. She is carefully considering telling Reza about tonight's planned dinner while riding up to Boston. Finally, she hears Reza shut off the shortwave. He comes out the door.

Akhtar smoothes her skirt as she climbs into the passenger seat. Reza holds the steering wheel as though it's a large tray.

After they have driven a few blocks on Boston Neck Road, just as they pass Twin Willows, Akhtar breaks the silence.

"Karbassi, she's invited someone besides us tonight . . ." She smoothes her skirt again. He still holds the wheel like a serving tray.

"Karbassi, did you hear what I said?"

"*Areh, areh*, Yes, yes, I heard you. What do you want me to say?"

"Nothing. I only thought you'd want to know who she's invited," Akhtar says, trying to sound casual.

There is silence.

Finally, Reza asks, "*Ki?*" He's looking straight into the traffic. "Who has she invited?"

Akhtar hesitates. Even though she'd planned this conversation while waiting on the lawn, she has fresh doubts. *Is it better to blurt it out and get it over with or ease him into the subject gracefully?*

"Well? Are you going to tell me who?" Reza asks again.

Now he's paying attention. Akhtar looks out the window at the houses.

"Are you going to tell me who?" He is losing patience.

"We haven't met her guest before."

"But did she tell you who they are?"

"*Areh*. And there's only one guest."

"Okay, tell me who this person is—who then?"

"His name is . . ."

A car honks and swerves in front of the van. The driver throws Reza the finger.

"*Pedar saag!*" Reza curses him. "Son of a dog!"

Akhtar notices that her husband has tightened his grip on the steering wheel. She looks down at her watch. The drive from Narragansett to their daughter's apartment in Boston is only an hour-and-half. *Will that be enough time to calm him down?*

"You see what I have to put up with—see how hard it is—driving the candy around for Dairy Mart?"

"*Areh,* Karbassi, I know it's hard," she acknowledges dutifully.

"*Khob*—Enough! Who is she inviting?"

"A boy."

"*Pesar?*" Reza asks, surprised.

"*Areh,* Karbassi, a boy." Their implicit rule has always been that their daughter cannot have a boyfriend. It is just understood.

"*Your* daughter has invited a boy?"

Akhtar immediately knows that Reza is furious. When one of his children earns his wrath, they immediately become Akhtar's child.

"Karbassi, she's twenty-two now, she lives on her own. And she's here, in *Emrica.* What is there for me to say to her?"

"There you go again making up excuses for your children. Tell me how long you've known about this."

He asks as though he's uncovered a conspiracy between his wife and daughter.

"She only told me when she called to ask us over for dinner."

"What has she told you about him?"

"Not much."

"Well, do you know his name?"

"*Areh . . .*" she says carefully, as if stepping over landmines. "She's told me his name."

"Well then?" He is browbeating Akhtar with his look. "*Esmesh chist,* what's his name?"

"Hadi."

"Hadi?" Reza shouts, "an Iranian?"

"*That's* an Iranian name," she says, her voice starting to quiver.

"Don't get wise with me! You two. You and your daughter. The pain she causes me—all her life. And—now! An Iranian boy!"

Reza runs through the litany of outrages he believes his daughter to have committed. Akhtar has heard it all before. She tunes it out.

"Does that girl of yours ever stop and think?" he says, looking over to his right.

"Karbassi, slow down!"

Reza brakes sharply.

"This must be one of Kambiz's friends?" he says, assuming that the only way his daughter would have had the opportunity to meet an Iranian would be if it's one of Kambiz's friends.

"No, she said she met him through her roommate."

"Roommate?"

"*Areh.*"

This silences Reza. For a while they simply drive. Reza holds a conversation with himself, muttering this and that, slapping the steering wheel every now and then. They pass the Warwick mall. They're nearly halfway there and Akhtar has more to tell.

"Hadi's from Hamedan," she says as calmly, as if she were observing the weather.

Reza pulls the car over to the shoulder and screeches to a halt in the breakdown lane. He slams the car into park and looks over to Akhtar.

"*Sharestooni?* From a province?"

Akhtar nods apprehensively.

"What does his father do?"

"She hasn't told me that yet," she replies, threading her fingers tightly together.

"What *did* she tell you then?"

"That she's invited someone named Hadi to dinner."

"And you didn't bother to ask who he is?"

"I'm sure we'll find out."

Reza's eyes flash back and forth. "We're not going. We're turning around right now! You needed to tell me this before we left the house."

"Karbassi, please." She grabs his arm so that he won't put the car back in gear. "Please. We're only going to a dinner."

Cars and trucks zoom by, shaking the van.

"We'll just go to dinner, there isn't anything more. They're not getting married."

"I have worked so hard for us to get our green cards," Reza shouts.

"What does this have to do with our green cards?"

"If it wasn't for those, we wouldn't be able to stay in this country."

"But Karbassi, they won't take the green cards away if she invites an Iranian."

"She won't ever become an American! Can't you get that? What kind of life can she have in this country? With an Iranian? *Sharestooni?*"

"I don't see what you're saying."

"She can never go back to Iran, why can't you see that?"

"You can't say that, Karbassi. If she married an Iranian, then it would be easier."

"What's left in that country for their generation? That country will never be normal again. Turban shit Khomeini won't accept a ceasefire with Iraq. That war will go on until he dies. Look at Kambiz—twenty-seven and running his own business. He can do that only here. This is America. What will they go back to in Iran? Prison? Executions? . . . I wish Keyhan had gotten out in time . . . why did he stay?"

The van sways side to side.

"And she has to find someone who is poor, ignorant— probably *mazhabi* too."

"I only said he's from Hamedan."

"THAT means he's *shahrestooni* . . . what do you think his father does? He's not licking stamps in some office. They don't have any. And, *mazhabi*—martyrs for Allah—that's all I expect from a *shahrestooni*."

"Look at us. We're sitting in a van. You deliver candy to Dairy Mart. I bake cakes, cakes that I make on our kitchen table and sell for a few dollars each. Who are *we* now? Has that ever occurred to you?"

"This isn't who we are; it's just temporary. How many times do I have to tell you?"

"Karbassi, please, just let's go. Last time you two got in a fight, you didn't speak with one another for three months."

Reza curls his lip.

"She's not like me, you can't force her to follow your rules like you do with me," Akhtar says.

Cars continue to race by. Akhtar looks outside the window. Maybe she shouldn't have said that.

"I'll go," Reza says.

"*Basheh*. Okay."

"But don't expect me to say a word."

"That's alright. She wouldn't expect you to say much."

Reza puts the van back in gear and merges into traffic. They drive the rest of the way in silence. At the door of her daughter's apartment, by way of a subtle reminder, Akhtar says, "Karbassi, please . . ."

Narragansett
2005

By late afternoon, the humidity clings to Akhtar like a leech. It's not like the dry heat of the desert—here in Rhode Island the humidity sucks out your energy. It's been a long day. There is still much to sort. She spots a broken television. Twenty-five years ago, the television featured the news from Iran every night. But after the American hostages were released, Iran faded from the nightly news despite the thousands dying in the brutal war with Iraq. After 1981, they looked for news in letters from their son Keyhan and from relatives. Reza still curses at the news on the shortwave radio.

Akhtar spots a bundle of envelopes tied together with a pastry box string. She flips through them like a deck of cards—return addresses in Farsi, variations of Mr. and Mrs. Karbassi in English with looping handwritten letters.

She examines each letter carefully. Are these letters worth keeping? Should she drag them all the way back home in her luggage? Would she ever read them again in Kerman? Does she need to remind herself of the years she endured? Should she keep them so that she can give herself a good, long cry? Why relive what's better forgotten?

She considers giving them to her daughter. Maybe they can be useful for the story she wants to tell. Her daughter never knew her grandfather, Sadegh. Would these short, perfunctory letters give her a window onto his life? Does holding his letters, with his crude and illiterate writing laboriously scratched onto paper, give her daughter a memory she's never had?

Could these letters help her daughter tell their story? Like the moon, the letters only show one side of the story. The letters may tell a lot about the sender, but will this help her daughter see the other side of the moon?

There will be nothing in these letters to tell her daughter how hard it has been for Akhtar all these years. How homesickness swells inside her until she feels the need to burst.

She should just throw the letters away. She slaps the bundle against her thigh. If only it were that easy. She thumbs through them.

She sees a letter from her son. "Keyhan *joon,*" she calls out, as if he had just walked in the door. She smiles. The sort of smile only a mother wears: proud, nostalgic, ever loving, braided in the colors of gentle mirth. A first born changes you, she thinks to herself, looking down at the letter bearing Keyhan's handwriting. She thinks back to when Keyhan was born.

Akhtar was barely eighteen. Keyhan was delivered by a midwife in her father's house in Kerman. Reza was working in Tehran. They had been married for a year and she was living at home while they saved up money for a place in Tehran.

Soon after he was born, Akhtar took Keyhan to Tehran and they settled into family life. Reza doted on little Keyhan. Haunted by the death of his brother Javad, from pneumonia, Reza made sure that Keyhan was always bundled in layers of clothing regardless of the season. He would check the baby's room for drafts and monitor his eating. If the baby failed to have a bowel movement, he would yell at Akhtar and blame her food for the baby's constipation.

As Keyhan grew older, Reza devoted more of his free time to his son. When he got home from work, he would wrestle with his son, rolling on the rugs, laughing. Reza would dig out two pot lids and the two of them would pretend to drive cars. Reza poured his love into Keyhan.

When they got back from London, Reza beamed with pride at the fact that Keyhan had learned English during their time there. He wanted the best education for Keyhan, enrolling him in Alborz, the best private school for boys in Tehran. He drove Keyhan halfway across the city to get him to school.

He wanted to give the world to his first born—the best education, the right career.

But it was not enough for Reza to want to give him the world, for the world is filled with hurdles that Reza could not manage for his son. The biggest obstacle for a young Iranian man of his class was the *concour,* the rigorous college entrance examination that instilled fear in families and their children. Annually, only 10 percent of those who take the test pass. The children of their friends and acquaintances who failed are sent away to colleges in France or England.

Reza wanted to prove that his son was one of the best. So he made a bet with Keyhan: if Keyhan passed the test, Reza would buy him a new car. Keyhan not only passed but scored among the highest. Reza was beside himself with pride. The next day, he bought Keyhan a navy blue, Iranian-made Paykan. They sat behind the wheel of his brand new car, Reza filled with joy.

Keyhan never was much of a letter writer. He wrote only a handful during their eleven long years of separation. When the Shah fled, Keyhan left Iran briefly, in January 1979, but returned when an interim government was formed by moderates. Like his father, he believed the chaos would be temporary. But that February, Khomeini arrived from France and soon thereafter, Iran became the Islamic Republic. When the airports closed, Keyhan was stuck. Many of Keyhan's friends were arrested, others executed. Keyhan knew he was being watched by the new government. Anyone with any connection to the Shah was suspect.

Keyhan withdrew from everyone he knew. The wrong association or a slight misdeed could land him in prison or worse. He didn't go to any of the funerals of his executed friends. He associated only with family.

Then came the war with Iraq. From the beginning, Iraqi planes dropped bombs on Tehran. Keyhan had more than his own government to fear.

Resting on a milk crate, Akhtar scans the envelope. It has got that yellow tinge of age; a rip here, a tear there. It bears the stamp of the Revolution—a silhouette of raised fists. Their arms raised above their heads, like a sign of defiance or even triumph, different from the simple crown emblem stamps of the Pahlavi era. She pulls out the letter and carefully unfolds paper, crisp like onion skin.

3rd of Azar, 1366.

She roughly translates this into the Western calendar as the fall of 1988—near the end of the eight-year war with Iraq. Iran's borders were still closed. No one was permitted to leave. Iraq continued to bomb Tehran.

She brings the letter closer to her eyes and begins to read:

Pedar o madar aziz,

I'm sorry that it's been a while since my last letter. My responsibilities with NIOC have become greater. They seem to dump more on me each day. It's not that cushy job I thought it would be when baba signed my employment papers. He was so excited that he was bringing me into the folds of NIOC like his Khan Amu Iranpour. These days, they keep sending me to the south. I've made several trips to Abadan. Our refineries have gotten a beating and I've been going down to supervise the rebuilding. I've seen some pretty bad devastation down there. Sadaam's planes hit a school a few weeks ago. Parents are still trying to find bodies under the rubble. It makes you wonder how people will survive this.

I'm not sure if you are following the news here but for the past few months the bombings have also reached Tehran again. We've put up black curtains and at night we're only supposed to have dim lights on in the apartment. They don't really help. The sirens still go on. Everyone in the building is accustomed to rushing to the basement to take cover. But we have heard about too many buildings collapsing atop the basements, killing those who had sought cover. Now we drive out of the city.

There's a biyabooni by Sa'adat Abad where we go to. Or we drive into the Damavand Mountains. We can see the city from up there. Once the shelling stops, I drive us back. I keep a jug of water, formula and blankets in the trunk. Some nights it drags on, and we fall asleep in the car. Sometimes it's gotten so bad that I've had to send Sholeh and Kiana down to Kerman: the south is relatively immune to the shelling. Aunt Soodabeh is there now with them.

At this, Akhtar stops reading and thinks back to the first time she heard the news that her son was getting married.

Keyhan's marriage to Sholeh was hasty. It had taken both Akhtar and Reza by surprise. Keyhan had been the model of progressive Iran—living a freewheeling bachelor life with many girlfriends. Why would he ever marry Sholeh?

Akhtar was getting ready for bed when he called. A telephone call at night is disturbing, but a phone call from Iran was unheard of in those days. It was too expensive. And talking to someone in the United States caused suspicion.

Keyhan spoke quickly. He had married his cousin Sholeh, the daughter of Reza's sister Soodabeh. To Akhtar and Reza it was unacceptable—a throwback to the old traditions of the rural villages. They were shocked. The conversation ended abruptly. Akhtar doesn't remember saying congratulations.

After the phone call, she and Reza sat silently in the dark of their room.

Reza finally spoke.

"I wish we had been there to block this marriage."

Several weeks later, they received a carefully worded letter from Keyhan. He began by telling Reza that his older sister, Aghdas, had died from ovarian cancer. On her deathbed, Aghdas had asked to witness the marriage of Keyhan and Sholeh. With the letter, Keyhan included a photograph of the wedding.

Keyhan and Sholeh stood beside Aghdas's sickbed. Around them were Soodabeh and Aghdas's children.

Over the years, Akhtar has surmised that just as Keyhan did not know how the Revolution affected his family in America, they could not understand how it felt to live in Tehran. At the chaotic time of the Revolution, Keyhan could trust no one but his family. He was thrown together with them in the chaos of reprisals, threats, and then war. He was the man of the family and carried the burden of protecting his aunts. Was there a comfort in Sholeh that Keyhan needed? Or did he marry her to satisfy a dying aunt?

Akhtar folds the letter and puts it back in its envelope.

Keyhan arrived at New York's LaGuardia airport on August 25, 1990. They drove from Narragansett to pick him up. The reunion was giddy with laughter as they drove home in the car—the whole family together after eleven years. Akhtar wanted the ride to last forever. Her three children were happy, kidding each other as if they'd never been apart. Reza wore a baseball cap and she poured tea from a thermos.

When they got back to Narragansett, the euphoria fell into deep sadness. Around the oval kitchen table, the tears flowed. For hours they all sat there not knowing what to say, or where to begin. So they just cried.

Keyhan stayed only a month. Reza pressured him to stay, to move to the United States permanently. "It will be a better life for you here," Reza pleaded.

"I've seen so much bloodshed, seen our country suffer so. I can't just give up after all we've been through."

"It will be easier for you here."

"How can you know? You didn't go through what we did." Sounding like Abolghassem, Keyhan said, "We have paid a price for that country of ours."

"That country is not Iran anymore—not the true Iran."

"You don't know Iran. Things are getting better. We're moving toward better times."

"Don't tell me I don't know Iran—"

"*Baba,* I don't want to end up in this country as a janitor. I'm treated with respect in Iran. I've been getting some of the best NIOC assignments. However bad our government is, Iran needs me. Our brains fled; they need people like me. They take care of me now."

"I got you a green card—aren't you grateful for that? Every Iranian is desperate to get out, they would kill for that green card—what's the matter with you?

"Why would I want to give up a good life and come here to work in a gas station? Look at you—you ended up with your Dairy Mart store and delivering candy. That's not a better life to me. I don't want to lower myself."

"Lower yourself! I fought for everything I have and you just take. You couldn't make it pumping gas—you don't have the guts."

Reza prodded Keyhan for ten years to come to America. In 2000, Keyhan moved his family to Fresno, California. He said he did this to be near Sholeh's brother. But, Akhtar senses that he chose it so that he'd be farther from Reza.

Keyhan called Akhtar from California last week.

On the phone, Keyhan sounded depressed. And resentful.

"You wanted me to leave Iran and come here and now you're going back? I thought you wanted me to be near you."

Akhtar listened. She didn't know what to say. She didn't mention that he was still thousands of miles away.

"You see what's happening to me," Keyhan said. "Just why I didn't want to come here—I have to grovel for a job. In Iran, they used to bow to me. Do you understand that?"

Akhtar nodded, the phone silent. She remembered the photograph of Reza kissing the Shah's hand and thinks how similar her son and Reza are.

Keyhan called again the next day. His back pains were getting worse, he said. They were sending him for more tests.

Akhtar had never known her son to complain about his health. She looks at her watch and wonders if she should call him to learn about the test results.

Then, pressing her palms against her thighs, she lifts herself off the milk crate, walks over to the garbage, and throws the batch of letters in the can.

Narragansett
1985

"To the right—no a bit more. It's the red box. Yeah . . . no, not that one . . . the red box . . . next to it, next to it . . . that's it. You got it." The customer is a heavyset man wearing a loose-fitting t-shirt, jeans, and sandals. "What are you—new here or something?"

Reza looks through his bifocals at the man and smiles. He has no idea how to find the right cigarettes. He places the pack of Marlboro's on the counter.

"Dat iz one dollar and eighty-five cents, sir."

"Sir?" the fat man smirks. "I've never been called *that* before." He slaps a dollar bill and some change on the counter and scoops up the cigarettes. The bells on the Dairy Mart door jingle as he goes out.

The fat man unwraps the pack of cigarettes and casts the cellophane on the ground. He slides into a rusty Chevrolet with a dented door and broken headlight. The Chevrolet careens out of the parking lot.

What a waste of money, Reza thinks, *the man does not drive a decent car but buys himself a package of cigarettes.*

He makes a mental note to tell Akhtar to sweep. The number of tasks he wants her to do are already beginning to pile up, so he reaches for a pen to make a list. Since he and Akhtar are the store's only employees—and he rightfully its owner—delegating tasks has been easy for Reza. Sliding himself onto a stool behind the register, he takes out a lunch-sized paper bag and scrawls several tasks in Farsi, raising his head frequently to scan the store.

In the summer of 1983, days after Reza received his green card—giving him legal residency and the right to work legally—Reza visited the headquarters of the Dairy Mart franchise. The offices were clean and organized. The salesman showed Reza the manual: step-by-step instructions on running a Dairy Mart convenience store. This is America, he thinks. Everything is organized: how to display the products, where to put each item, when to mop the floor, when to put money into the drop safe.

Reza proudly signed the contract papers with Dairy Mart.

That night, he told Akhtar.

"Karbassi, we don't know a thing about running a store in this country." Akhtar was nervous.

"What's there to know? You stand there and sell stuff." He held up the official Dairy Mart management manual. "Americans are organized, they know how to do these things—right down to the smallest detail—smooth and efficient."

Akhtar sat across from Reza at the oval kitchen table. She clasped her hands and nervously twisted her ring. "Karbassi, this is a lot of work."

Reza shrugged his shoulders and scratched the back of his neck.

"What do you know about work?" he said.

"It's like this house. You think there is no work . . . but there is always work! How can we manage this store?"

"Khanom! Don't be ignorant. The register will tell you how much change to give. Now you want to tell me you no longer have a brain?"

"I'm afraid of what you've gotten us into." Her voice drifts away . . . she loses her voice when upset. "You say it has to be open from five in the morning to eleven at night? Who is going to work these hours?"

For a moment, he thought about her point. Their daughter had recently moved to Boston for work, Kambiz was struggling to start his own business, and Keyhan was still stuck in Iran. There is no one to lean on but themselves.

"It's easy. I'll work the morning, you work the afternoon, and I'll come back and close the store at night. Later on we can hire someone."

"Seven days a week?" she asked.

"So you earn a little bit of cash baking cakes—now you think you can question me?" Reza exploded. "What are we going to do? Survive on baking cakes?!" He pounded his fist on the table.

Silence.

With trepidation, Akhtar asks, "Karbassi, how much do we have left?"

"It's none of your business how much I have. What does it matter anyway, it's all frozen in Iran. All of it. My savings account used to earn 20 percent interest back then. Now it's all gone. What option is there?" His voice is as somber as the dark room upstairs where he spends most of his time.

"Karbassi, can't you get a job, maybe one of your NIOC contacts would know how to help . . ." Akhtar regrets asking as soon as the words come out. She knows her husband is far too proud to turn to his former colleagues.

Reza just scratches the back of his head.

"*Basheh,* Okay," Akhtar gathers from Reza's silence. "How about applying for a job, like one of those that they list in the newspapers?"

"You forget that I'm fifty-nine years old and spent thirty years working for the NIOC. Which American company is looking for someone like me? Huh? Have you thought of that? Any other smart ideas from you tonight?"

Akhtar doesn't dare suggest the option of going back home. She already knows that by getting political asylum, they had shut that possibility out.

Two women walk up to the register. Reza slips off his stool and stands erect. Straight and stiff-backed, as though the Shah's entrance was just announced. The older woman, wearing heels and a skirt-suit, puts a gallon of milk on the counter.

"Excuse me!" It is the younger woman—college age with a ponytail and sweat suit.

Reza smiles and gestures to the older woman. "Why can't she wait her turn?" he thinks.

"S.O.S. Where is the S.O.S.?"

"By the window." Reza points to the aisle. He begins to ring up the gallon of milk.

"S.O.S? There's no damn S.O.S. here."

The young woman comes back to the register.

"Where's the S.O.S.? Come on!"

"Miss, I told you—all the medication is over there."

"Medication? No, no, S.O.S. You know—the scrubbing things!"

"Vat scrubbing tings? S.O.S. is emergency."

"Oh my God. You're serious! Hey, just forget it." The young woman heads to the door. "Jesus, damn foreigners."

Reza watches her leave. He looks at the woman in high heels. "Vat was dat?"

The woman pushes the milk toward him. "How much is this? I don't have all day."

"Yes, yes, miss, dat is von dow-laar and nine cents. Tank you."

She hands him a twenty dollar bill. She taps her car keys on the counter while Reza makes change. He sees her watch—a Rolex.

"Dat's a very nice watch, Miss, like mine." Reza pulls back his sleeve. He is wearing a silver Rolex, a trophy from his days of working for NIOC. "I am very proud of this."

She grabs her change and leaves without a word.

Reza hears her high heels click on the bright linoleum floor. "Should I have said goodbye?" he thinks. No one would leave without saying goodbye or thank you. "Why didn't she say anything?"

He bought his watch when he was on top of the world—working in New York for the Shah's oil company. People said to him "yes, sir" and "thank you, sir." He was the one who was served and told people what to do—ever since his early days in the oil fields of Abadan barking orders at the peasant laborers. "Does this woman think that she is better than me?"

He thinks about the customers that day. The fat man was a nobody. The college girl was rude. But, this woman in high heels had money. "She doesn't know about me."

In Tehran, Reza remembers how he and his colleagues would leave the office at midday to drive to the top of the Damavand Mountains, the home of Rostam and the mythical heroes of ancient Persia. They would take lunch there, looking down at Tehran. They were in the clouds, and Tehran was an anthill below them. By day, they were building the new, modern Iran. At night, they would drink Scotch, eat caviar, and plot their next moves while their wives lived a life of *poz*, one-upmanship: making sure that everyone knew who had the most servants to complain about.

Here, he is nobody.

No one is in the store now. He takes a sip of tea from a Styrofoam cup. "Why think about it?" Though the tea is cold, he continues to drink it.

The Dairy Mart door jingles and a white-haired man with an old fisherman's hat comes in. He pours coffee from the pot. "I can only have half a cup these days," he announces from the back of the store. The old man strips the top off of four creamers, fill up the rest of the Styrofoam coffee cup. He dumps in four packets of sugar.

"Beautiful morning, huh?" the old man says when he reaches the counter.

"Yes, sir." Reza responds, although he hasn't even noticed the weather today.

"Don't call me sir, call me John," and reaches his hand over the counter for Reza to shake.

"Tank you, John." Reza wonders what he should do next. John's clothes are old, but the man is friendly.

"And what can I call you?" John asks.

Reza pauses. He does not want the strangeness of his name to ward off this friendly man.

"Michael," Reza says suddenly.

"Michael?" John seems surprised.

"Yes, you can call me Michael."

"Michael? Where're you from?"

It has been five years since the Iranians freed the American hostages. The nightly news no longer shows Iranians chanting "Death to America." But, still, that's all most Americans know about Iran.

"I'm from the Middle East," Reza says.

"The Middle East—pretty big part of the world. What country would that be?"

"Persia," Reza says deliberately, using the country's ancient name. It doesn't carry all the hate, he feels.

"Eye-ran used to be called Persia? Right?"

Reza nods his head apprehensively.

"That's fine, that's just fine," John says. "Never been there myself, but I am sure it's a fine place."

John takes a sip of his coffee and pulls a dollar from his pocket.

"Well, it's a pleasure, but I best be going. What do I owe you?" John says, pushing the dollar bill across the counter closer to Reza.

"No, no, you my guest today." Reza slides the dollar bill back on the counter. It would be ungracious of him to take money from a man who just presented himself as a friend.

"Hey, Michael, that's awful decent of you. Thanks. Maybe I'll see you tomorrow."

Until the Revolution, Iran made Reza proud. The mere mention of his country drummed up nationalistic pride. Like his watch, Iran meant success and prosperity. It was home. Now he hides from Iran. Now, he is Michael, not Muhammad Reza.

"A man came to the store today—he reminded me of my friend Allen," he told Akhtar that night between shifts. The man has the same American style of easy camaraderie. Polite and civilized. Reza wonders, whatever happened to that prosperous relationship between our nations? Americans like Allen used to work in our country. He thinks of the days Iranians used to emulate these Americans.

Even as he works at the Dairy Mart, Reza continues his love affair with all that's American. He treats Americans with respect. He calls them "sir" and "miss." What would his grandfather, Abolghassem, think of his reverence for America? He would have whacked him with his wooden staff and said, "America is young. We are an ancient civilization. We must teach the young. Look toward your own nation, son, not a foreign one in the West."

But now? Iran is in the grip of bearded fanatics. Reza knows it's not a place for him.

"Hey, how you doin'?" It's a short, skinny man with a Pepsi baseball cap and a heavy Rhode Island accent. "I gotta delivery. You wanna open your back doo-h, mista?"

It takes Reza a moment to understand this accent. It is thick and incomprehensible. "Yes, vait pleaz," he says, leaving the cash register unattended to head toward the back area.

While Reza holds open a heavy metal door, the delivery man rolls in a hand truck stacked with a half-dozen brown boxes. Pushing the boxes onto the concrete floor of the delivery area, he hands Reza a sheet of paper on a clipboard for him to sign. This is Reza's favorite task. He enjoys signing the delivery confirmation papers. It gives him the feeling of authority he once had with his NIOC job.

The delivery man pops his chewing gum. For a moment, Reza is standing in his posh Tehran office, about to sign a document while his secretary politely waits. He relishes the moment. There is no delivery without his signature.

He hands the clipboard back to the driver.

"Okay, fella. You're all set. Have a good one."

"Have a good one?" Reza thinks. "Which one is good? Which one should he have?"

Back in the front of the store, a middle-aged woman is waiting impatiently by the cash register.

Throughout the year, Akhtar and Reza work from 5 AM to 11 at night. They come and go, passing each other in between their shifts. At first they work seven days a week. Fatigue sets in, though neither complains. Their son and daughter start to work on weekends. Kambiz likes the Sunday shift, when he can read the *Providence Journal.*

The days pass in monotony—a relief in light of the danger in Iran. Reza's new friend, John, comes in regularly, and the two discuss politics over coffee during the store's quiet, late morning hours. "You see John . . ." Reza will say with his accent, giving his American friend a beginner's course on Iran's political history.

A trendy, upscale restaurant, Basil's, opens up next to Dairy Mart, and its owner persuades the police station across the street to clear up the crowd that typically hangs in the parking lot. Reza sees the owner at night when they both close up. Basil's owner often invites them to come for dinner, but Akhtar and Reza never have time, nor can they afford it.

By the end of their first year, Reza's worries less about money. In Iran, the war with Iraq continues intensely. Iran is ravaged by hyperinflation and a depressed economy. Reza continues to think that the days of the Islamic Republic are numbered. He plans that they will run Dairy Mart until the "bearded fanatics" are defeated and Iran opens itself back up for self-imposed exiles. It won't be long, he confidently assures himself.

The waters off Narragansett Beach are gray and choppy with rising whitecaps. The afternoon skies have blackened, and the wind stirs the waves higher. The beach is deserted, the streets are empty. The coming storm has cleared the town.

Thick raindrops begin to pelt the picture windows of the Dairy Mart. Inside, the fluorescent lights give off an eerie, artificial glow. Akhtar is hauling heavy milk crates to load the dairy display case. Reza is home napping. He has left Akhtar a long list of things to do.

For a moment, Akhtar feels lightheaded. She leans against the picture window. The storm has intensified and rain is coming down in sheets now. She can no longer see the sea across the street. She rests a moment longer. Then back to work—there is so much to do. As she pushes herself, her body finally surrenders.

She faints by the large, glass fridges. A customer finds her sprawled across the linoleum floor and calls an ambulance. Akhtar is rushed to South County Hospital. The emergency room doctor discovers she has been hemorrhaging for over a month.

By the time Reza makes it to the hospital, the doctor has decided that she needs an immediate hysterectomy. She and Reza do not fully understand the operation. They are both scared. But, the doctor seems calm and certain. She is scheduled for surgery the next day.

Reza puts Dairy Mart's "Closed" sign up on the front glass door. Kambiz rushes down from Providence to stay by Akhtar's hospital bedside. He stays with his mother around the clock until her health improves. Reza calls Iran to tell Keyhan about his mother's operation.

Her daughter neither calls nor comes down to see her at the hospital. Akhtar thought that she was too afraid to see her in a hospital. The same fear is in all of them. Akhtar may seem a meek woman, but her daughter feels that the sole pillar of their support is close to collapse.

And Reza is scared. Akhtar's surgery brings back the pain of his childhood—the death of his father, mother, and brother.

Akhtar slowly recovers in the hospital. The Dairy Mart remains closed. On the day of her release from the hospital, as they drive toward home, Reza tells her, "I am giving up the Dairy Mart franchise."

**Narragansett
2005**

Akhtar can hear Reza's distant shortwave even from the garage. Outside, the afternoon sun beats mercilessly.

She continues packing, though more slowly now because of the heat. She is sweating, beads of it rolling down her forehead. She stops often to fan herself with whatever is at hand: a back issue of *Iran Times,* a placemat from Asia, last week's supermarket circulars, a dish—even box flaps.

She spots a box of mugs left over from her daughter's wedding. Each guest received a mug, and the excess ones remain here in the garage. She has one by her bed stand and another on the kitchen windowsill, both filled with dried pussy willow branches.

Akhtar blows the dust off one of the mugs and gives it a quick polish with the edge of her t-shirt. Her son-in-law designed these mugs. Using the flowing curves of Persian calligraphy, he wrote his name alongside her daughter's, one name leaning into the other. It looks like two flames burning into a new center—a single candle born of two.

Reza and Akhtar meet their daughter's friend, the young *Shahrestooni,* in Boston on that early summer night in 1984. Before her daughter opens the door, Reza expects to see his nightmare come to life—a bearded, *mazhbi* fanatic with a prayer-stone mark on his forehead.

Instead, Hadi is clean shaven and he works for the computer giant, Wang. For the first time since arriving in the United States—where he has been since coming to Shaw Prep in 1978—Hadi has money for new clothes, a car, and enough left over to send money to his father in Hamedan. No longer is he swiping ketchup packets from McDonalds' to squeeze onto white bread. He is no longer sleeping in shifts on an old mattress on the floor. After six years of desolation, long hours, and hard work, he feels a sense of satisfaction—almost euphoria. He is becoming the success he'd promised himself he would be.

The dinner is tense. Watching her husband, Akhtar almost holds her breath. She can see what he is thinking. Reza is tight-lipped during the dinner.

But not later at home.

Reza curses Akhtar. "Your daughter! Your daughter! You brought her into this world. I never asked for this girl to be born," he shouts.

Hadi seems the symbol of the Revolution to Reza, as though Hadi himself had thrown out the Shah and ruined Reza's life. And now his own daughter is turning her back on him.

"I gave her an American education. She dresses like an American girl. Her friends are all American. She talks like an American—she barely speaks Farsi. What does she see in this boy from Hamedan?"

Akhtar trusts her daughter to see her own way. Her daughter has a new interest in learning to speak Farsi. She has begun listening to Persian music and studying Iranian history. But does her daughter understand the expectations Iranian men have in marriage?

After several months, Hadi comes to dinner at their home in Narragansett. Akhtar prepares traditional dishes and the dinner conversation is held in Farsi. At one point during the dinner, Hadi abruptly excuses himself and goes outside. He is gone for a long time, and when he returns his eyes were red: to be with an Iranian family has stirred up such homesickness that all the tears he has held back for six years came rolling out.

Reza continues to confront his daughter about Hadi, as do his sons. Hadi is not someone they want to associate with, let alone call family. But his daughter is as stubborn as they are. She stands her ground in every argument, no matter how they tried to diminish Hadi. For once, Akhtar is glad to see her daughter's stubborn streak. Inwardly, she cheers her on as Reza hurls profanities at her for hours on end. She used to think that Reza was venting his anger over the Revolution on Hadi, as if he were personally responsible. She has tried to reason with him, but it never makes a difference. Reza never listens to her.

Looking back, Akhtar realizes that it took years before Reza came to accept Hadi. She can't say there was a magical instant when her husband saw the light, but he eventually conceded. It was a slow evolution—much like his conceding to go back home. His growl eventually gave way to a stubborn pout, his stubborn pout to a tight smile. Page after page turned until Reza finally came to terms with his daughter's choice. In those early years after Hadi had stepped into their lives, Akhtar was wary of what Reza might say or do. She was always on edge, worried that her husband would turn the whole thing back into the mess that it had been. It was as if Hadi stood on a mountain ledge with Reza ready to shove.

Narragansett
1990

Noruz, the Iranian New Year—literally "new day"—is celebrated on the first day of spring, the vernal equinox. It is the time of new life after the dying of winter. It is the oldest Persian holiday, dating back two thousand years to the time of the Zoroastrians. Iranians prepare by cleaning the house from top to bottom. This signals to the ancestral spirits that they are welcome to visit. Iranians spend the day in celebration visiting between families.

Forty years ago, on Noruz, Reza Karbassi returned to the streets of Kerman, his hometown, to meet face to face with his new father-in-law and complete the wedding contract. All of the marriage negotiations had already taken place. Reza had offered a mehr, a bride price of 15,000 tomans (approximately $45,000 in current value). Sadegh graciously accepted without making a counter offer, saying, "It's only a token to symbolize marriage." Sadegh believed that his daughter would never need her mehr. She would never leave a marriage that he had ordained. Though it is a bride's right to claim her mehr at any time, Sadegh knew that Akhtar would fulfill her duty as a wife faithfully and without disobedience.

In early March 1990, as she does every year, Akhtar covers lentil seeds with a wet cloth, placing them in a sunny window to get them to sprout—a symbol of prosperity in the New Year. She puts the sprouts in the center of the Noruz Sofreh, along with a fragrant hyacinth, apples, coins, a mirror, a candle . . . all symbolic of rejuvenation, light, and hope. Akhtar also places a Koran, while Reza places the wine; she honoring her faith, Reza his cultural roots. And as he does every year, he repeats, "Don't forget the wine Khanom! Don't forget we are Persians before we are Muslims."

* * *

In 1990, Noruz falls on March 21, as it often does. After the Noruz feast, Reza retires to his yellow chair. He dozes off while Akhtar does the dishes.

The phone rings.

"Khanom—phone!" Reza shouts.

"Reza—Iran—for you." Reza comes to the kitchen. He looks at Akhtar, but she says nothing, just holds the phone out to him. It is 4 AM in Iran.

Reza listens intensely, saying little. Akhtar watches him closely for any sign of bad news. A telephone call at night can only mean bad news. But she detects a slight smile on Reza's face.

"Who is it," she hisses. Reza motions for her to be quiet.

He punctuates his end of the conversation very briefly, nodding and saying, "*baleh*, yes," or "*basheh*, okay."

Then all of sudden, he seems to catch fire.

"Sell my daughter? I am not going to sell my daughter—do you take me for a barbarian? We did that a thousand years ago—we are Persians, *agha*, not primitives. I no more own my daughter than I own the sky over Hamedan."

Akhtar smiles. It is Hadi's father, Ahmad Khalili, calling on behalf of his son to ask permission for their daughter's hand in marriage. Reza is offended by the offer of *mehr*. He begins to lecture Ahmad. As usual, Reza looks as if he will explode in rage.

Then abruptly, he stops. Akhtar holds her breath.

"*Yes.* I will tell you yes, on one condition—do you hear me?"

There is a pause.

"*Baleh,* she can marry your son *only* if there is no bride price—no *mehr*," he shouts loud enough to be heard across the world.

The wedding date is set for September 1, 1990, but the parents give their blessing on March 21—on Noruz.

The couple wants a traditional ceremony.

Akhtar begins cooking a month before the wedding. How she yearns to have this wedding in Iran. She would be joined by all the women of her family, her friends, and her neighbors.

She thinks about her Iranian friends in the States, women she knows from the glory days of NIOC, the extravagant days of the Shah. They are now the wives of exiled generals and business tycoons. Yet they still live for *poz*—wearing designer outfits, talking about their vacations homes long since sold, and now, more than ever, exaggerating the number of servants they once kept. Their world—the majestic white stucco mansions on the sycamore-lined streets of northern Tehran—is gone. Now their husbands, like her own, sit penniless at home.

She can't call them *sameemee,* intimates; she can't see Khanom Jandaghi or Khanom Khosroshahi stirring rice pots or baking bread.

She yearns for the warmth and clutter of family, the noise and excitement that went through her house as everyone pitched in to help with preparations, relatives coming and going. But she has no choice—she is alone. She cookes and bakes for a month all by herself. She makes trays and trays of baklava and platters of *shirin polo* (Persian sweet rice) and *fesenjoon* (chicken pomegranate and walnut stew). She fills many dozens of grape leaves, *dolmehs,* by hand.

She cries as she cooks. She cries tears of joy for her daughter and her new son-in-law. She weeps for her home in Iran. She wipes her eyes steadily to keep her tears from falling into the food, which could bring bad fortune.

Hadi also feels a deep longing for home and family as the wedding approaches. He invited his elderly mother and father, but how could they come all the way from Iran? How could they even get a visa? There are still no diplomatic relations between the U.S. and Iran.

The nearest American embassy to Hamedan is in Istanbul—a 24-hour bus ride from Hamedan. Hadi sent money for his parents to travel to Istanbul, but they speak no English and have never been out of Iran. How could they explain why they needed to go to the United States?

They arrive in Istanbul and are greeted by long lines outside the embassy. They wait . . . too long for an elderly couple. When they finally make it to the head of the line, Ahmad gestures with his hands, trying to portray how desperately he wants to see his son, a son that he has not seen for twelve years.

The immigration officer looks at the two, perplexed, but he swiftly stamps the passports. They receive a three-month tourist visa.

The room with the yellow chair is full of flowers and the scent of wild rue incense wafts through the air. The incense is burning to ward off the evil eye. The *sofreh-ye aghd,* a beautiful silk cloth, is spread out on the floor. The guests are guided to their places around the *sofreh.* The bride enters. She kneels at the head of the *sofreh,* facing east, toward the sunrise, toward the light of life. Hadi is the last to enter, dressed in a dark suit and tie. He takes the place of honor to the left of the bride. Before him is the *aayeneh bakht*—a mirror with two candelabras that his mother brought from Hamedan. It is the same aayeneh bakht that his parents used for their wedding. The mirror and the candles bring light and fire for their future life together. The groom looks into the light and then into the mirror. He sees the face of his bride reflecting back.

Akhtar and others hold a silk cloth over the heads of the bride and groom.

Ahmad is chosen to reads the vows by virtue of his knowledge of poetry and religion. By tradition, after the groom agrees to accept his bride, he asks the bride three times for her assent.

The bride and groom sip honey to ensure the enduring sweetness of life.

Narragansett
2005

Akhtar turns the mug over in her hand. "September 1, 1990" reads the inscription.

How many mugs can she keep? How many does it take to shelter the memory? Each mug is full; she keeps each one. In Kerman, she will arrange them on her kitchen window sill, to remind herself of a rare good memory of her life in America.

Chapter 11
Iran

In July of 1988, Ayatollah Khomeini reluctantly accepts a truce with Iraq, saying he has "drunk the cup of poison" by doing so. He dies nearly a year later. Seyed Ali Hoseyni Khāmene'i succeeds him as the Supreme Leader, and Ayatollah Akbar Hashemi Rafsenjani, from a background of wealthy pistachio farmers in the province of Kerman, becomes Iran's fourth president. The hard line of the government of the Islamic Republic seems to shift during this time. Rafsenjani moderates the tone of politics; expatriates are invited back to help rebuild the war-torn country. Iran begins to shed its rubble as construction surges, and the economy improves somewhat. The sound of music, forbidden under Khomeini, can again be enjoyed, now that the radio stations play it. Women dare to don veils in colors other than black.

The pace of reform continues to hasten. In 1997, President Khatami is elected in a landslide election. He further softens the tone of Iranian politics, paving new roads between Iran and the outside world.

The world begins to embrace a new Iran.

Early in 1998, an American wrestling team is invited to compete in Tehran. Some of the American players do not wear the American flag on their uniforms. Yet, they receive great applause in the arena, second only to the Iranian team. For the first time since the inception of the new Islamic regime, an American flag is unfurled in Tehran without being burned or desecrated.

Later that year, the Iranian soccer team plays the United States in front of 65,000 World Cup fans in Lyon, France, where, for the first time in twenty years, Iranians publicly wave the Iranian flag. The Iranian players give each American player a single-stem rose. Then the Iranians give the Americans a real shock. They beat them, 2-1.

In 2000, the two countries meet again for another soccer match. Reza watches the game with his daughter and others. Tears roll down his cheeks.

Gradually word comes that some of Reza's former NIOC colleagues have traveled to Iran. Some of these colleagues had been blacklisted in the early days of the Revolution. Now they visited without being arrested and were able to return to the United States. Some even recovered property that had been seized during the Revolution.

Then, in 1992, Reza's own daughter goes back.

* * *

Growing up, I fought a lot with Baba. One of our fights was about me wanting to go back to Iran. I remember the shouting match we had over it. By this time, I was married to Hadi and Baba had fine-tuned his verbal attacks to include my husband as well. The first thing he blurted out when he learned of my plans was, "HE's the one who put you up to this, isn't that right? He's brainwashed you, hasn't he?"

"Baba, you're ridiculous. I've always wanted to go back, at least for a visit!" I didn't tell him about the dream I recently had of Tayebeh. How my grandmother stood behind a glass door, her ember-colored sweater still hauntingly vivid in my mind. That would have only made matters worse. Baba would say I've lost my mind.

"There's nothing there for you—nothing but a bunch of filthy mullahs whose minds are in the gutter. What do you think is back there waiting for you? Opportunity?"

"I just want to know who I am. Every time someone hears my name they ask, 'Where are you from?' I am never sure what to say. I am Iranian, but what does that even *mean* to me? I want to go back to understand myself. To see the country that I was born to . . ."

"I'll tear up your birth certificate if you go." He turned to my mother and said, "Khanom, get me her birth certificate."

"What does a birth certificate have to do with this? Besides, that's not going to stop me, Baba!"

Our typical post-fight anger silences remained intact right up to my trip. Baba didn't come to the door to see me off. Moman held an *Aeeneh Ghoran*. I kissed the Koran (not knowing one word of it) and she splashed water at my heels and blew a *Van Ye Kad* prayer after me.

I'm sure Baba yelled plenty at Moman while I was away.

I was gone four months. I sent home many letters, with photos. I wrote Moman and Baba and told them I had gone to the cemetery where Sadegh and Taybeh were buried. I knew how much that would mean to Moman (she had still not been able to go back to visit their graves). I described Kerman to them, how Khaje-Khezr, where Moman once lived in a mud house, had since been laid over by a road.

I think those letters turned a cement wall to a glass door.

When I returned from my trip, Baba listened carefully. I could tell he had softened. I could tell he yearned to open that glass door, too.

Iran
1999

The plane flies over the Damavand Mountains, with Tehran below, and lands at Mehrabad International Airport. A short, balding man drops to his knees on the tarmac and cries out *"Vatan!"* Homeland. Reza's first step on Iranian soil draws a similar emotion, though he forcefully holds in his desire to do the same.

Armed soldiers patrol the terminal leading to passport inspection. There is an eerie silence. Tired passengers cue up for customs under the white wash of fluorescent lights.

Reza grips his maroon Iranian passport. He begins to sweat nervously in line. Everything is so different that he is unsure if he has come to the right country. He is worried that things might yet go wrong. He thinks the government is too unpredictable. A litany of worries run through his mind: What if he is not as lucky as the friends and colleagues who have come and gone? What if they hold him up? His political asylum could still make him suspect. How long will they keep him in jail if they do arrest him? Will he end up dead? He scratches the back of his neck.

When he reaches the counter, the customs officer is young. He could not have been more than a child at the time of the Revolution. He wears the thick, Islamic beard—*mazhabi*. Reza knows that even a quick examination of his passport tells his story. He left in 1978—before the Revolution—and has not been back since. He draws in his breath as the officer flips through the pages of his passport. The officer arches his eyebrow and looks at Reza.

"You've been away for a long time, *agha*." Slamming the passport with a stamp, he slides the passport across the counter to Reza. "*Khosh amadid, agha.* Welcome home, sir."

Two days after leaving Akhtar in Narragansett and after spending one day in Tehran with Keyhan, Reza arrives in Kerman. Though it is only May, the desert breeze is hot, laced with the smell of jet fuel. Behind him waiting to deplane is a line of women in veils—chadors of grey, brown, or black—and one of unshaven men with collarless shirts. None of the men wear ties; that symbol of Western culture is visibly erased. Everyone is in a hurry to get off the plane.

Reza halts at the top of the boarding steps. He grabs the stair railing, but the steps are so narrow. His heart races and his hands tremble. Is it his Parkinson's disease or is it fear? he wonders.

"*Agha,* please keep moving," someone says to him from behind.

"*Pedar,* father, let me help you." A bearded young man gently takes Reza's arm and guides him down the stairs. The young man patiently helps Reza clear the last step and Reza gives a quick nod of gratitude. It is the second time that a *mazhabi* man—whom Reza distrusts by their appearance alone—has helped him.

Reza walks slowly. The other passengers hurry past him. He is fatigued and stressed. He stops before the glass door leading to the terminal. He takes off his bifocals and wipes his eyes—brushing away tears or fatigue, he isn't sure.

It has been fifty years since he's last been in Kerman. Twenty-one years since he has been in Iran. He had vowed never to return. He left Kerman when he was twenty-two, and his final time in Iran was when he was fifty-one. Now he is seventy-two. The Iran he loved has changed—has been polluted and twisted in the name of God. Still, he is home now.

The glass door leading to Kerman's terminal slides open to reveal a flock of people waiting for their loved ones. Someone rushes past him and calls out "Moman!" Reza sees a black chadored woman waving her hands. Wearily, Reza steps forward.

There are more than thirty people waiting to welcome Reza: cousins, nephews and nieces, even some childhood friends. All five children of his older sister, Aghdas, are there. They are all adults now with spouses and children of their own. There is his cousin Eisa with his wife and three children. He proudly tells

Reza that he's named their youngest after him. There are Akhtar's brother and his family, Reza's high school friend Ohadi, and a few of Akhtar's cousins. The faces are familiar but older. There are some he's never met. Many kiss his hand, others hold him tight. The children stare at him in awe—the relative from the United States.

Before heading toward the parking lot, there is much discussion. Who will get the honor of driving Reza to Parvin's house? Parvin, as the eldest niece, gets to host Reza.

One of Reza's nephews, Masud, points out a framed photograph hanging on a marble column in the center of the lobby. Reza slips his bifocals on, but still can't quite make out the photograph. Masud takes Reza over for a closer look. Reza has seen the picture before. He has a copy in his family album in Narragansett. At the center of the picture is his grandfather, Abolghassem, wearing a jet black robe and turban, carrying his wooden staff with his chest raised high.

The caption reads: *One of Iran's greatest masters of Persian carpets, Abolghassem (Karbassi), next to an expansive carpet that took his team of weavers four years to complete.*

By now, the trailing family entourage stops to wait for Reza, who is firmly planted in front of his grandfather's photograph. Passersby look about oddly at the large group huddled around Reza—an old man who is staring at an insignificant photograph in Kerman's small airport. Reza, with the weight of age bearing down on his shoulders, is gazing beyond the photograph into his memories. He stands there feeling humbled.

In the photo, Abolghassem's look is proud, defiant. Reza feels that his grandfather's eyes are looking right into him. His grandfather and father fought proudly for their country. Abolghassem was courageous—he endured prison for his beliefs. His father, Mahmoud, fought the British, living like a bandit in the mountains. Would they say that he deserted his country, hiding in his room in a foreign land?

Is he worthy of the name Karbassi? Reza wonders.

Masud gently tugs his arm. The families are waiting to drive him to Parvin's. There are stories to tell and food to be eaten. As with any family, there are tears to shed—for the past and for the future.

Reza pauses for one last look at Abolghassem. He thinks he hears a voice—a whisper. "Home," it says. It's time to come home . . . for good.

Narragansett
2005

It is nearly six o'clock in the afternoon now. A slight breeze off the Atlantic Ocean makes its way across Boston Neck Road and into the garage. Stretching her back, Akhtar takes a deep breath, wipes her forehead with the back of her hand, and glances at her watch. Reza will be asking for dinner soon. It's time to quit for the day.

She looks around to see if she's made any progress. She sees Reza's photograph with the Shah. Reza is still kissing the Shah's ring and the Shah is still staring off into some distant future.

Through the hallway—the windowless passage—she steps, her eyes adjusting to the dim light of indoors. She hears the crackling noise of Reza's shortwave in the living room, all too recognizable, predictable as the hands of a clock. It frustrates her that, like an idol worshipper, her husband sits upon that yellow chair listening to that radio. For hours. Obsessed to hear the scratchy news from Iran. Some time ago, by way of consolation, her daughter proffered a reason why Reza has sat upon that yellow chair of his all these years, listening to the shortwave. She told Akhtar that, for her, the connection lies in the *color* of his chair. Yellow, her daughter said, symbolizes the return of a loved one. Or perhaps in Reza's case, *toward* a loved one. Akhtar looks into the living room and sees Reza slouched forward, half-dozing, half-listening, half-there. She wonders if there's any truth in that.

I'll be glad once that piece of metal rests in the trash, she thinks. If there's one item in this house she would get rid of without reservation, it's that radio. If only the events it had announced for all these years could also be disposed of . . . all the terrible news it brought to them. Maybe she's blaming the messenger, she thinks, shrugging her shoulders. Still, she feels good to know that she'll be throwing it away soon.

In the kitchen, she pulls a plastic bag of long-grain rice from the cupboard. Scooping two measuring cups of rice, she pours them onto an old saucepan. The grains stream down like heavy sand. She runs water on top of the grains until it turns milky white. She dances her fingers through the rice to stir it.

She wears a gold ring with a carnelian stone in an oval setting, a gem from a bygone era. The ring belonged to her mother, Tayebeh. It has been fifty-six years since Akhtar left home. She thinks of her mother and her wisdom every day. For any situation, Tayebeh could summon a proverb for guidance and comfort.

What would Tayebeh have said about her life in America? What would her mother, who never saw anything but the desert, say of the lush green lawns of Narragansett? What would she say if she had seen Rhode Island's deep blue, shimmering ocean? What wisdom would Tayebeh draw from her daughter's half-century of *ghorbat,* away from homeland and family?

She pours fresh water over the rice and places it on top of the stove's small burner, turns it on high, and waits for the water to boil. She has done this nearly every day of her married life.

She feels she hears her mother's voice:

Azizam, Auseman-e har koja hamin rang ast—the color of God's sky is the same color everywhere.

A ripple begins to gurgle on top of the rice.

* * *

It is windy. Gales blow dust across the unpaved streets of Kerman. She keeps her head tucked down inside her chador to avoid the gritty wind. She is afraid. She doesn't want to look up. She has a lump in her throat and her legs feel heavy. She is walking beside her father, Sadegh.

She glances up at him. Even with the sand swirling around, he looks straight ahead and keeps a steady pace. For the entire walk, he doesn't say a word.

They are walking to the mahzar, the office, to sign her marriage contract in front of a mullah.

Just outside the office, Sadegh stops abruptly. He clears his throat. Akhtar also stops, pulling aside the fold of her veil to look at him. She quickly looks away. She grips her veil tightly as the wind whips her chador. Like a bird sensing a cage, her veil flaps its wings ferociously against the wind to free itself.

Father and daughter stand side by side for some time, with only the empty wind whistling between them.

"Akhtaroo . . . in life you will have to learn to endure . . ." Sadegh speaks haltingly in the wind. "Bacheh jan, dear child, remember, for the sake of your future family . . . you must endure."

Akhtar drops her head, seeing only her father's weather-beaten black shoes.

* * *

The rice water comes to a boil. Akhtar continues to stir.

Steam rises from the boiling water. She scoops up a single rice grain and gently presses it between her fingers. There's a slight hardness at the center that only an experienced hand can detect. She removes the pot from the heat and pours the rice into a colander. She then spoons the drained rice back into the pot and drops slices of butter on top and watches it melt. She takes a small bottle of saffron and pours a bit over the rice. The grains turn yellow.

"Agha, I did endure."

She looks into the rice and sees Sadegh's torn shoes.

She hears Reza's radio again.

Karbass is the strong burlap of Kerman woven to endure, the name that Abolghassem took for his family.

Endure—that is what I have done.

She closes the lid over the rice.

"Michael" Reza Karbassi
May 1, 1927 – August 15, 2011